CHILDREN LEFT BEHIND

THE DARK LEGACY OF
INDIAN MISSION BOARDING SCHOOLS

"*Children Left Behind* is a sad story of a nation's best intentions gone awry. Tim Giago's personal accounts reveal an untold tragedy of abuse of helpless children by those who had the responsibility to protect them. To fully understand the calamity, you need only to visit the graveyards of the old boarding schools and see the hundreds of graves of Indian children who did not survive the misguided assimilation efforts."

Richard B. Williams
Oglala Lakota, President & CEO, American Indian College Fund

"*Children Left Behind*, written by respected journalist Tim Giago, is a fascinating mix of personal stories and history about the role of government and mission boarding schools in the lives of Native people. The book provides the reader with the cultural and historical context for many of the problems encountered by Native American families in the early 21st century."

Wilma Mankiller
Former Principal Chief of the Cherokee Nation

"*We were separated from our cultural and spiritual teachers, our parents and grandparents. We were beaten physically, psychologically and emotionally for being Indian. Our culture, language and spirituality had to be stripped away so that we could become cheap imitations of our mentors, the Franciscan nuns and Jesuit priests, prefects and brothers...*"

"*...There are few Indian families who have not experienced the residual impact of the abuse heaped upon their friends and family members after they were victims of the rape and abuse they experienced at the hands of the missionaries sent out to save their souls. It was not only a sin, it was a crime.*" (*Tim Giago*)

CHILDREN LEFT BEHIND
THE DARK LEGACY OF
INDIAN MISSION BOARDING SCHOOLS

BY TIM GIAGO
NANWICA KCIJI
ILLUSTRATIONS BY DENISE GIAGO

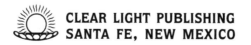

CLEAR LIGHT PUBLISHING
SANTA FE, NEW MEXICO

Copyright 2006 Tim Giago
Clear Light Publishing
823 Don Diego
Santa Fe, New Mexico 87505
www.clearlightbooks.com

First Edition
10 9 8 7 6 5 4 3 2 1

Library of Congress Cataloging-in-Publication Data
Giago, Tim A., 1934–
  Children left behind : the dark legacy of Indian mission boarding schools / by Tim Giago (Nanwica Kciji, Stands Up for Them).-- 1st ed.
     p. cm.
  ISBN 1-57416-086-9
  1. Off-reservation boarding schools--United States--History. 2. Indian children--Education. 3. Indian children--Abuse of . 4. Indian children--Crimes against. 5. Catholic Church--Corrupt practices. 6. Racism in education--United States. 7. Racism--Religious aspects--Catholic Church. 8. Christianity and culture--Moral and ethical aspects--United States. I. Title.
  E97.G53 2006
  371.89'97073--dc22
                                                    2006002980

Original paintings © Denise Giago
Historic photos © Tim Giago
Cover painting © Denise Giago
Cover design: Marcia Keegan and Carol O'Shea
Interior design & typography: Carol O'Shea

This book is dedicated to all of those former students who went through the rigors of the Indian mission boarding schools and urvived with their language, spirituality and culture intact.

This book is also dedicated to Lydia Whirlwind Soldier, a Sicangu Lakota from the Rosebud Reservation. She not only survived the trauma of St. Francis Indian Mission Boarding School at Rosebud, but became one of the wonderful poets and educators who helped to define and bring an end to this horrific experiment in Indian education. Lydia recently retired from the staff of Todd County Schools on the Rosebud Reservation, where she was a strong influence in Indian Studies at the reservation schools.

It is also dedicated to Charlene Teters, a member of the Spokane Tribe of Washington state and an instructor at the Institute of American Indian Arts in Santa Fe, for her undying struggle to end the use of the Indian people as mascots for America's sports teams. She has often been called "The Rosa Parks" of Indian country by her many friends and admirers. Charlene is a gifted artist in her own right.

And finally, the book is dedicated to my lovely daughter Denise Giago, an Oglala Lakota, a graduate of the Institute of American Indian Arts, who illustrated this book. Denise also illustrated my book *Notes from Indian Country, Volume II* and together we are a team. I believe she will soon make her mark in Indian country as an artist and as a filmmaker.

TABLE OF CONTENTS

PART II: FROM THE DISTANCE OF TIME

EPILOGUE

FOREWORD

Imagine, if you will, the most extreme, repugnant abuse you can think of. For some who experience this treatment, they may never get over it. The trauma is forever too close to the surface to allow sweet forgetfulness to take hold. These individuals live daily with dark memories of their shocking abuse. For many, there is no healing. Their painful experiences affect in countless ways their education, their work, their relationships, their families…their entire lives. For some, there is no escape other than suicide. For others, the toll can be counted in the divorces, joblessness, alcoholism and drug abuse, child and animal abuse, crime, and on and on.

Others who suffered the same experiences may have memories just as painful, but their manner of dealing with them is quite different.

Such is the case of Tim Giago, the American Indian author who for ten years suffered at the hands of Catholic priests, prefects and nuns at Holy Rosary Indian Mission at Pine Ridge on the Pine Ridge Reservation in South Dakota. Giago was exposing these appalling stories long before it became trendy to report on clergy abuse of the young. In a book of poetry and in his weekly newspaper columns, Giago has been focusing attention on this revolting chapter of U.S. history for almost three decades.

It all began 100 years ago as an experiment to acculturate and assimilate Indian children by forcing them into boarding schools operated by the Bureau of Indian Affairs and several Christian churches. The system produced far more bad results than good, even though Giago is quick to point out that some of the nuns and priests were wonderful teachers who instilled in him a thirst for knowledge.

The original idea, Giago writes, was to "kill the Indian to save the child." Sadly, too many children were figuratively, if not literally, killed.

Each fall on U.S. reservations, Indian boys and girls were taken from loving homes and placed in boarding schools. For the next nine months they were punished for speaking their native language in class, forced to attend Mass six days a week and twice on Sunday, made to sleep on Army cots in cold dormitories and given watered-down mush to eat. Boys and girls were segregated, and any interaction was strictly controlled. In effect, they were being indoctrinated into white, Christian customs.

Giago poignantly relates the sadness of leaving his home to go off to school, and the happiness of his mother returning to take him home at the end of the school year. He tells how some Indians got their names, and he writes with humor about how some classmates got nicknames. And, of course, he relishes in explaining the system boys used to send messages to girlfriends on the other side of the school, and vice versa. When it comes to young love, where there's a will there's a way.

However, there is only disgust in the tales of sexual abuse and in the reaction of a sadistic priest to discovering that the boys had befriended a stray dog and cat.

The experiment in boarding schools ended in the 1970s, and since then the Indian people have struggled to put in place an education system that allows students to speak their native language and places an emphasis on teaching the real history of the Indian people. In that vein, Giago, a much-honored journalist whose Indian name, Nanwica Kciji, means "Stands Up for Them," says it is now time for healing, and he offers an olive branch to those who sought to protect a seriously flawed system.

It is time for those on the other side to take a step toward healing the wounds they created.

E. Ray Walker
Op-Ed Editor
Knight Ridder/Tribune News Service
Washington, D.C.

INTRODUCTION
SPEAKING FOR THE ONCE-SILENCED VOICE

The true history of the Indian Missions and Bureau of Indian Affairs boarding schools has never been written. At one level, it is a part of the legacy of America's efforts to acculturate and assimilate the Indian children of this country. But at a deeper level, it is a history of shame.

Beginning in the middle of the 1800s and continuing until the 1960s, boarding schools were established across America, starting on the East Coast with schools such as Hampton Institute in Virginia and Carlisle Indian School in Pennsylvania.

Strangely enough, although there were Indian tribes in the East, most of the students at the early boarding schools came from the Indian tribes of the Northern Plains, the Southwest, Kansas and Oklahoma.

The boarding school I attended for ten years was the Holy Rosary Indian Mission at Pine Ridge on the Pine Ridge Reservation in South Dakota. The school changed its name to Red Cloud Indian School in the 1970s.

The Indian Historian Press, Inc. in San Francisco published *The Aboriginal Sin*, my book of poetry about Holy Rosary Mission, in 1978. After the book went to different media outlets for review, some of the journalists reviewing the book called Holy Rosary Mission to ask questions. They were told by some priests that I had attended HRM for only six months and by others that I had never been a student there. The priests who gave out this misinformation did so with a clear conscience because when I attended the school it was named Holy Rosary Mission. After the name was changed to Red Cloud Indian School, the priests

Tim Giago's class at Holy Rosary Indian Mission in 1949. Giago is fifth from left, top row.

could say, with tongues in cheeks, that I had never attended Red Cloud Indian School.

Nearly everything about my school years was erased. Even photos in yearbooks suddenly disappeared. According to the records at Holy Rosary Mission, I was a nonperson who had never attended school. I had to get affidavits signed by former HRM students like Gerald Clifford to prove I ever went to school there. Clifford wrote, "I definitely remember Tim as a student at HRM during most of my school days there and although he may not have attended Red Cloud Indian School, he did attend Holy Rosary Mission."

Why would Catholic school officials try to erase me from the records? They took umbrage at the poems I wrote about my school days at HRM and became frightened because I had exposed many of their deep secrets. They also felt that this small book of poetry would damage their ability to solicit contributions. In fact, the superintendent of the school asked me to write a letter he could send out to his contributors attesting that things had changed dramatically at the school since I wrote the book of poetry. He never bothered to ask me why I wrote what I wrote.

Writing *The Aboriginal Sin* occurred quite by accident. But then again, when one has the deep-seated beliefs of the Lakota, perhaps it was preordained. This is how it started.

When I joined the U. S. Navy in 1951, I had bouts of depression and oftentimes the bouts led to memories of my school days at the Mission. I started to write poems about the school and about the friends I made there and about the priests and nuns. I saved the poems in a shoebox and kept adding to them as the years went by. Nineteen years later I opened the box and found it stuffed to the top. I typed all of the handwritten poems and sent them to Rupert Costo, a Cahuilla Indian man who was editor of the Indian Historian Press, Inc. in San Francisco. A few weeks later, I got a phone call from Rupert, a man who had also attended an Indian boarding school, and he said, "Tim, these poems have got to be published." We came up with the title, "The Aboriginal Sin," because the Mission I had attended was operated by the Catholic Church and the play on words referred to the biblical teachings of original sin. In the Catholic Church the original sin was one bestowed upon all infants, and they carried this sin until they were baptized into the Church.

Rupert published the book in 1978. Of course, this was long before the scandals that rocked the Catholic Church in the 1990s.

The Aboriginal Sin is now out of publication. Before Rupert's death in 1987 I bought the copyrights to the book. The book was sold out everywhere it was carried, and I still get requests for copies.

In 1981, I started a weekly newspaper on the Pine Ridge Reservation that I named *The Lakota Times.* I had been writing a weekly newspaper column since 1979 for the *Rapid City* (SD) *Journal,* and I often expanded on the poems in the book and wrote about HRM in my weekly column. After I started my newspaper I continued to write weekly columns for the *Journal.* Eventually, however, I pulled the column after the editor accused me of "Catholic bashing."

Many of these columns were included in my books *Notes from Indian Country, Volumes i and ii.* These books were compilations of the columns I had been writing since 1979. Jessie Sundstrom, a wonderful lady who had been the editor of the *Custer* (SD) *Chronicle,* took on the task of preparing *Notes from Indian Country, Volume i.*

The dark history of the Indian boarding schools was a subject that main-stream America knew little about. But I have always believed, and the passing years have served to enforce that belief, that the damage done to the Indian people by the boarding schools was so severe that it is a part of our problems even today. The schools set about trying to destroy a culture, centuries-old traditions and worst of all, the inherent spiritual-ity of a people. Along with that came the efforts to destroy the native lan-guages of the students. We were forbidden to speak our native tongue under the threat of severe punishment.

The policy of the government- and church-operated boarding schools assumed that by housing us in institutions nine months of the year, sep-arating us from our traditional teachers, our parents and grandparents, denying us the social environment that was a powerful part of our cul-ture, and immersing us in Catholicism and social reform, we would become totally Americanized.

But in order to accomplish this we had to be indoctrinated into believ-ing that our ancestors were nothing more than heathens and savages and that we were now offered the opportunity to become better than that. In other words, our past had to be erased so that we would have a future.

The consequences of attending the boarding schools have been dev-astating. In their efforts to paint our ancestors as less than human, the schools managed to create very low self-esteem in us. By subjecting us to the heretofore unknown experience of corporal punishment, the schools passed on to the students a streak of cruelty that manifested itself when the young Indian boys and girls moved on to maturity and started to raise their own families.

The physical, psychological and sexual abuse of many students became a part of their normal routine, and they took these horrible les-sons into their private lives after leaving the boarding schools. I saw this in my own family. My younger sister, Shirley, was raped at Holy Rosary Mission. She was violent and cruel to her own children all her life.

These are the girls of Holy Rosary Mission in 1914. Tim Giago's mother, Lupe, is in the second row from the top, third girl in the row.

One cannot severely abuse children and not expect that these children would take that form of abuse into their adult lives. It is now a commonly known fact that the abused often become the abusers.

I believe that there is not a single generation since the late 1800s that has not experienced the legacy of violence as victims of the boarding school graduates. Rampant alcoholism and drug abuse afflicted many boarding school graduates and was often passed on to their descendants.

In Indian country, it really didn't matter whether the Indians of today ever attended the boarding schools themselves, because nearly every one of them had an aunt, uncle, mother, father, grandmother or grandfather who had been a victim of the boarding school system. Many suffered the extreme problems of collateral damage.

Another terrible outgrowth of the boarding schools was the lack of parenting skills and the inability to have long-term relationships, a consequence that was experienced by so many former students. Without the lessons to be learned from our parents and grandparents because of the forced separation, Indian students had no role models to emulate. How to interact with their peers as they matured and how to interact with their own children in later life would have been a part of their natural, cultural growth in an Indian community. Cut off and denied access to their traditional way of life, the children became victims of what I call "cultural imperialism."

Sex education at a Catholic Indian school? Forget about it. The subject not only didn't exist, it was taboo. On the rare occasions when it was brought up, priests and nuns pointed out all the evils and sins of sex. Even comic books of the scantily clad Wonder Woman were verboten and always confiscated. The boy or girl unfortunate enough to be caught reading one was severely punished. This sexual suppression manifested itself in many ways later in the lives of the boarding school students.

The Bureau of Indian Affairs boarding schools were just as problematic although religion was not the focal point. One BIA teacher was charged, in the 1960s, with assaulting more than 300 Navajo boys and girls. But in all of the boarding schools, destruction of the culture and the language were high on the list of educational tools used to de-Indianize the students.

To be torn from the loving homes of our Lakota parents and then to be placed in a cold, cold institution was in and of itself extremely traumatizing. Beyond that, to be placed in an environment where all teachers and related staff were not only white but also Jesuit priests and Franciscan nuns could also be terrorizing.

When I was a boy we were in the middle of the Great Depression. Even though my parents had been products of the boarding schools, the extreme poverty on the reservation made the schools an alternative to starvation. They felt that we would at least have a roof over our heads and three meals a day.

I grew up in the Pejuta Haka (Medicine Root) district of the Pine Ridge Reservation, and we seldom saw non-Indians. This was true of many of the students who ended up in the boarding schools. The sudden transition was a frightening experience for all of us. Suddenly white people—who were

The Giago family. Tim Giago is in the front row, far right. Top row: Sophie, Shirley, Lupe (mother) and Mary Jane. Bottom row: Tony, Lillian, Ethel and Tim.

also our disciplinarians—surrounded us. And their style of discipline went against everything that was a part of our culture.

When my father, Tim Sr., and my mother, Lupe, attended Holy Rosary Mission at the turn of the century, attendance at the boarding schools was mandatory. BIA police often visited the homes far out in the districts of the reservation to apprehend children, often from the loving arms of a mother or grandmother.

My grandmother, Sophie Abeita, was the descendant of a Sioux mother and Isleta Pueblo father. Her father, Antoine Abeita, had come to Dakota Territory in the mid- to late 1800s on one of the annual cattle drives that brought beef to the people of the Great Sioux Nation as part of the Treaty of 1851. He met a Lakota woman named Lucy Good Shell Woman, my great-grandmother, married her and settled down on what would become the Pine Ridge Reservation to stay.

Poverty on the Indian pueblos of New Mexico was extreme, and the Indian people there had been subjected to Indian mission educations under the Spaniards long before the Lakota people. The cattle drives that started in Texas and wound their way through New Mexico afforded the men of the Indian pueblos a chance to get a job and to leave some of the poverty in their own lands.

My grandfather on my father's side and my great-grandfather on my mother's side came to Dakota Territory from the Indian pueblos in New Mexico. My great-grandfather on my mother's side, Demetrius Tapio, married a Lakota woman named Holy Woman and spent most of his life in Dakota Territory, although he did return to his New Mexico roots on occasion. He was from the Pueblo of San Juan in Northern New Mexico.

Many of the cattle drovers who came to Dakota Territory from New Mexico married Lakota women and settled in and around Kyle or Pejuta Haka. They ranched and farmed along the river known as Three-Mile-Creek, and the area soon became known to the Lakota people erroneously as Mexican Creek. It should have been called Pueblo Creek because the drovers were men of the Indian Pueblos who acquired their Spanish surnames from the Conquistadors.

Soon many of these drovers became integrated into the Lakota society. Their descendants married Lakota men and women and they lost the ability to speak their native languages. The Lakota language became their language and over the years, their Pueblo blood became minuscule as they became total citizens of the Great Sioux Nation.

Just as the boys and girls of the South Dakota boarding schools often had their Indian names changed, so too did the boys and girls of the Indian pueblos under the Spaniards.

The Bureau of Indian Affairs (BIA) had a big hand in name changing. Agents were sent out to the different districts on the reservation and they would write the Lakota names of the inhabitants down, bring them back to the Agency headquarters at Pine Ridge Village, and interpreters, or Ieska as they were known by the Lakota people, would translate the names. The name Ieska soon became the word for mixed blood and the Lakota with Spanish surnames became known as Spiolas.

When the Indian agent recorded my family name he took the Spanish Pueblo name of my grandfather, which was Gallego, pronounced guy-ay-go, and put it down phonetically as Giago. Because there were several thousand Lakota on the Pine Ridge Reservation, translating the names into English often became a tedious task. The Ieska, along with their white supervisors, often grew weary by the end of the day and rushed the interpretation of the names. They frequently just made up names to get the job done more quickly and often they made up names with terrible meanings.

One family was named Stinking Thighs and another Two Belly, and they even went so far as to name one family Urinates Beside the Road. These insensitive interpreters didn't stop to think that these Lakota people would forever be labeled by the names they bestowed; indeed, they were often urged on by white supervisors who cared even less.

But the Indian missions and BIA boarding schools cleaned up the names and often shortened them. The Brave Heart family became the Heart family. Years later they would change it back to its original name, Brave Heart. When an Indian joined the military he or she again had name problems. For example, when Enos Poor Bear joined the U. S. Army during World War II, his name became Enos P. Bear because the middle part of his name was taken to be his middle name. Poor Bear went on to become the president of the Oglala Sioux Tribe and he designed the flag that is now the official flag of the Oglala Lakota Nation.

Many who read *The Aboriginal Sin* when it was published in 1978 assumed that I was attacking the Catholic Church, and some took umbrage at the book, including some of the former students of HRM who had become devout Catholics.

It was never my intent to attack the Church, but the methods it used in an effort to Christianize and "whitemanize" us bothered me. I found them much too harsh; they left us with such low self-esteem that when we left school and went out into the real world, we struggled mightily to find out who we were and what was expected of us.

Many of us had to re-educate ourselves because so much was kept from us. For instance, although the village of Wounded Knee was only about twenty miles from HRM, we were never taught about that horrible day in 1890 when nearly three hundred of our relatives were gunned down by the men of the Seventh Cavalry.

We never learned that students at HRM, including my grandmother Sophie, had to feed and water the horses of a contingent of the Seventh Cavalry when they rode on to the Mission grounds, tracking down Lakota who had fled Wounded Knee.

It is ironic that many of the boys and girls who attended the Indian Mission boarding schools went on to have productive careers. The discipline and the education we received took hold in many of us despite the hardships. But thousands of others lived out their lives as alcoholics, drug addicts, wife abusers, child abusers and worse.

The Indian Mission boarding schools had a profound impact upon my life and they were one reason I became a writer and journalist. I must have been a pretty good writer even as far back as the sixth grade. My teacher then was Mr. Fagan, a prefect who would soon become a Jesuit priest. After grading a paper I had written he accused me of plagiarism.

I was taken aback because the piece I had written originated in my own mind. Mr. Fagan said at the time, "As a writer you will never amount to a hill of beans."

Perhaps, subconsciously, I set out to prove him wrong. In 1991 I was awarded the Honor Award for Distinguished Service in Journalism by the University of Missouri School of Journalism. At the luncheon that day the moderator asked the recipients of the awards, "If you could have anyone in your life seated at your side this day whom would you choose?"

When my turn came I stood up and said, "I would choose a teacher I had in the sixth grade at Holy Rosary Indian Mission who once said that as a writer I would never amount to a hill of beans." A few years later I ran into Father Fagan and he not only remembered his remarks to me, but he apologized to me for making them.

Many of the graduates of the boarding schools who went on to receive a higher education returned to the Indian reservations to help bring an end to the boarding school system. They also pushed the schools to integrate many of the subjects that were forbidden under the old system, including the Lakota culture and language.

St. Joseph's Indian School in Chamberlain, SD, published an advertisement in my newspaper apologizing to the Indian people for its treatment of Indian children. This does open the door to healing, but the Catholic Church and its hierarchy have never apologized. I believe that in order to continue the process of healing, an apology by the Church must be a prerequisite.

A lawsuit against the Catholic Church and the United States government that was started a couple of years ago on behalf of Indian children appears to be going nowhere because of statute of limitation laws. I don't think that money would ever make the difference, but it will take more than an apology to bring an end to a time that uplifted and at the same time nearly destroyed a people. Many of us have healed ourselves but have gone through terrible personal tragedies in order to reach that point. Even those who believe the boarding schools have never impacted their lives know deep down that they did.

This book is intended to bring back the memories of the boarding schools to those who have survived them. It is also intended to cause those memories, good and bad, to bring about a process of healing that has long been denied. But more than that, it is written to bring out the truth that has been hidden for too many years.

In a traditional Lakota ceremony held many years ago, after I returned from Korea, I was given the name Nanwica Kciji by Enos Poor Bear and Grover Horned Antelope. The name means "Stands Up for Them" and it is a name I carry with great pride since it was given to me long before I became a journalist.

Many Lakota people who attended boarding schools have told me that my articles about the Indian Mission experience have proved to be cathartic for them. Some have said the articles helped them to heal. This has served to reinforce my belief that the Indian boarding school experience goes much deeper than many of us ever realized.

But make no mistake. The construction of schools, oftentimes hundreds of miles from the reservation homes of the students, did not happen by accident. Why else would a government or a religious denomination assume control and direction of these mortar and brick establishments and soon fill them with innocent children?

In reality, the collusion between church and state to systematically attempt to destroy a culture through education was no accident. The "do-gooders" who thought up and implemented this vast experiment knew exactly what they were doing, and they truly believed they were helping to save a people rather than destroy them.

In this book, I have incorporated many of the columns I wrote about Holy Rosary Mission over the years. My daughter, Denise Giago, provided new illustrations, and the book has grown from the small book of poetry I wrote in 1978 to include many of the memories that have occurred to me since then. I have often received calls from former boarding school students who reminded me of things that happened at the school that I had long forgotten. These, too, are now part of the book.

I recall speaking to a Lakota woman who became a Catholic nun. She said the book of poems caused her to take a really hard look at herself and her choices and made it possible to accept who she is and what she wants to become.

It is for these reasons that I am rewriting and expanding *The Aboriginal Sin,* now titled *Children Left Behind: The Dark Legacy of Indian Mission Boarding Schools.*

Tim Giago
Rapid City, South Dakota

PART I
AT HOLY ROSARY MISSION

PRELUDE
SHADOWS OF MEMORY

THE MISSION SCHOOL
It stands like a gothic city,
Red bricks and grey concrete,
In the middle of the Dakota plains
On the Pine Ridge Reservation.

The Jesuit Fathers of the Society of Jesus
Built this bastion of Catholicism in the late 1800s
To spread the religion of the righteous.
I stood last summer at the cemetery,
High on a hill above the church,
And looked at the rows of graves
Of the fathers, brothers and sisters.

So many of them came from Europe
To serve as missionaries in the wilderness,
To save the souls
Of primitive, savage heathens.

We were as alien to them
As they were alien to us.
They smiled in paternal benevolence;
We scowled in fear and distrust.

Perhaps they didn't save our souls.
But did our souls need saving?
Sometimes they found a convert
As we shook our heads, bewildered.

And now they lie in tiny little rows,
Names chiseled in cold granite,
Flickering names, long-forgotten memories
Of a time not so long ago.
When I pass a Catholic church
Sometimes I remember them,
Not always with fondness, I fear.
But I never enter the church.

GONE, BUT NEVER FORGOTTEN

There is nothing that can make a man feel that he is an ancient relic more than being asked by a high school student, "What was it like back in the old days at the Mission?"

Of course, the young fellow was referring to the Holy Rosary Indian Mission, which so many Lakota people attended on this reservation. Back in the old days, the Mission was a boarding school, and we not only attended classes and religious indoctrination sessions but lived there nine months out of the year.

His question did stir some memories.

I remember lying in the top bunk of the Army cots we used in the dormitory and listening to the last-minute guffaws and whispers that floated about the huge dorm just after the lights went out.

The prefect who supervised our dormitory would put up with our noise just briefly. He would then, in his most authoritative voice, tell us to knock it off. We all knew he had the wherewithal to back up his command with force if necessary, so we usually piped down and settled in for a good night's sleep.

To me, this was one of the worst times of the day. All of the schooling, praying and playing was over and now we rested in our bunks with only our thoughts. Mine usually drifted to my parents living out in Kyle on the reservation. I wondered what they were doing, and it was at times like this that I missed them the most.

Usually we fell to sleep listening to the squeaking shoes of the prefect as he attempted to walk silently up and down the aisles between the rows of bunks. I often wondered why the prefects, in their long black robes, could not wear a pair of shoes that did not squeak when they walked. A cough, a sneeze, someone mumbling in his sleep, and the irritating squeak of the strolling perfect were the last sounds we heard before drifting off to sleep.

At long last, the deep sleep awarded to active children would embrace us and—at least for the night—we were secure in our little world.

In the wee hours of the cold winter mornings, when the steam heaters that lined the walls become silent, the chill in the dorm caused most of us to curl up in little balls, roll as tightly as we could into our Army blankets, and fall into the deep sleep that comes with the approach of dawn.

Suddenly, like a splash of cold water thrown in our faces, the shocking clang, clang, clang of the large bell carried in the hand of the prefect would shake us from our slumber. He would walk up and down the aisles clanging the bell, and if he thought his message to wake us up was not having proper effect, he would stand over the bunks of those who had not hit the deck and clang the bell directly into their ears. By this time the dorm lights were on, and we would stagger sleepily from our beds and wash our faces from a row of metal basins. Then we would walk down the flights of stairs to the little boys' gym and fall into ranks, awaiting the command to start marching into the dark morning to the chapel for morning Mass. We repeated this scenario seven days a week and twice on Sunday for nine solid months of the year.

All the boys and girls had jobs. Some of the boys worked in the shoe shop, carpenters' shop, dairy farm and so on. The girls did the laundry and helped prepare the meals with the nuns. I am sure they had other work also, but since we were separated from them I have no knowledge of these jobs.

Under the supervision of Coach Bob Clifford, a Lakota man, I became the school's barber. I would start with the first graders and cut hair all the way to the seniors and by then it was time to start all over with the first graders. I made a lot of extra money cutting hair while I was in the Navy.

When the potato crops came in or the apple crops, all of the boys, no matter how small, participated in the harvest. We also cut the sugar cane that grew in the fields of Mission Flats.

The clothing we wore when we first reported to school was taken from us and stored in what we called The Cloak Room. We got our good clothes back on Sunday mornings for Sunday Mass. Our regular clothing was bib overalls and chambray shirts for the smaller boys and jeans and chambray shirts for the older boys.

This routine was repeated seven days a week. The only break in the daily activity came on Sunday morning. On this special day we got to sleep until the sun came up.

I think the longest hour of the day was the hour we spent in church each day. We clutched our prayer books and obediently mumbled the Latin responses expected of us. We moved restlessly to shift weight from our aching knees. I think most of us actually looked forward to Holy Communion because it gave us the opportunity to get up, stretch our legs and take a little stroll up the aisle. We also knew we were reaching the end of church services by the time Communion rolled around.

Well, at least this is one perception I have of the Mission. And the young man was right. Looking back on it now, it does seem like ancient history. But I think that somewhere, way out on the many Indian reservations of this land, there are those—like myself—who feel it happened only yesterday.

SIX DAYS A WEEK AND TWICE ON SUNDAY

Boy, the dormitory was cold at 6 a.m.,
As the first clang of the bell, hand-carried by the
Black-robed prefect up and down the aisle,
Resounded in our ears.
We dreaded the feel

Of the icy floors
That would meet our bare feet
And send us shivering
To the basins of cold water
And the smelly soap
Placed in rows
In the long troughs
That served as sinks.

Outside it was pitch black,
And our shoes made squeaky sounds
In the powdery snow.
We marched in company columns
Through the holy arches
With our hands jammed deeply
Into our warm pockets
And blanched at the thought
Of dipping our warm fingers
Into the icy Holy Water,
And feeling the cold cloth
Rub against our legs
As we genuflected
In reverence.

Monday through Saturday,
Six days a week,
And we enjoyed it so much,
We did it twice on Sunday.
You should have seen
Those beautiful callouses we developed
On our knees
Because every time we shifted restlessly,
Or tried to relieve the weight,
We were soundly cautioned

By the nuns and prefects
With a saintly smile.

Across the aisle from us
Segregated like holy cows,
Sat the lovely girls.
I don't know who invented it,
Could have been Bozo
'Cause he was always doing crazy things...
But suddenly one fine morning
The monotony of the sanctimonious drone
Was softened by the fine art
Of sparking.

Now sparking wasn't confined to boys,
Because we heard rumors that the girls
Were getting quite adept
At this lovely pastime.
First you found a small mirror
That you could easily conceal
And placed it secretly in your palm.

You used it like a rearview mirror
To gaze upon innocent girls
Seated demurely across the aisles.
And if you caught their eye,
You boldly winked.

Sunday mornings, we'll never forget.
They let us sleep 'til it was daylight outside.
And we got to wear our suits.
No more prison-issue clothes,
But good suits and ties.

And although we all knew
That Sunday Mass was longer
Than a weekday service,
We also knew
At the end of the Mass
We'd troop to the dining room
For our Sunday morning treat...
Cornflakes.

INDIAN DANCING
We weren't allowed,
To think Indian,
To speak Indian,
Or to be Indian...
Until late one spring.

The dancing contest began
When the grass turned green,
When the ice began to melt,
When the birds came back,
Always late spring.

The winners were chosen
To dance in New York,
To dance in the city,
To raise lots of money,
All they could bring
Back to the Mission...

Much people to please,
Much cash to be raised,
Much dancing to praise,
Until next spring.

INDIAN SCHOOL DAYS — AND NIGHTS

END OF SUMMER, END OF FREEDOM

When I was a boy, I would start getting that queasy feeling in late summer. I knew soon my dad would be packing us up and driving us to the boarding school where we would live and go to school for the next nine months.

One year, I waited until I knew my dad was all ready to head out and then I hid out in the tall weeds, hoping I would be overlooked and left behind. Dad missed me immediately, of course, and he marched to the edge of the field where I was hiding and told me in no uncertain terms that I'd better get my behind to the car or I'd be using a pillow for a chair for the next two weeks.

His threats were enough to bring me out of hiding. I made a quick dash for the car, ducking a couple of mean shots from my dad aimed at the back of my head. My mom chipped in with "Don't hit him on the head, he's crazy enough already."

My brother, sisters and I were all wearing stiff new clothing. Each of us had a pocket filled with new coins given to us by our dad, I suspect to ease our pain at being sent to the boarding school.

My money would be turned over to the prefect in charge of the candy store to be entered into a ledger, which would permit me to buy candy and have the cost deducted from my savings until the money ran out. It usually lasted me an entire two weeks. From then on, or at least until Christmas, my coffers were bare. This was great for your teeth, but mighty rough on your self-esteem.

My new clothes would be taken to the "wardrobe" or laundry room, as we called it at the boarding school, and turned over to a nun to have our names written in indelible ink on patches sewn into the clothing.

We were issued school clothing, which we dubbed our convict clothing, and our new personal clothing was put into storage to be handed out on special occasions.

The saddest part of this annual adventure was saying goodbye to our parents and then watching them as they drove down the long, dusty driveway to the blacktop highway. This was usually when the king-sized lump in my throat gave way to a flood of tears.

One year a boy raced after the car that had dropped him off shouting the name of his aunt. Her name was Eunice, but he was such a small boy that all he could scream was "Hoonis." To this day he bears this nickname. We all tagged him as "Hoonis." Of course, Hoonis now has a "Doctor" in front of that name.

After of a summer of my mom's good home cooking, the first meal in the dining hall was almost nauseating. For dinner we usually got a plate of strange-looking soup, bread and a cup of watery tea.

We were issued bedding and assigned a bunk in the boys' dormitory. After sleeping at home, usually three or four to a bed, the bunks with their straw mattresses seemed like lonely places, and when the lights went out that first night at school, you could hear some of the younger boys crying themselves to sleep.

It was during the first two weeks that the runaways headed for the hills in the greatest numbers. Sometimes we were organized into hunting parties to track down some of these kids, whose only crime was that they missed their family and wanted to go home. Oftentimes the chase was by men and the older Indian students mounted on horses.

My friends Peter and Alonzo Two Bear were usually the first to run away. Once I heard a Jesuit priest telling a new prefect to keep a close eye on those Bear brothers because they would turn rabbit in a day or two.

We spent the first two days readjusting to the boarding school life and renewing old friendships. Of course, when you reached high school age, that meant checking up on the girlfriend you had last year. Since the girls were segregated from us, this meant smuggling a note to your girl through the underground mail system, the laundry baskets that were hauled to the girls' side each day.

It took me about ten days to get over the queasy feeling, but as all growing boys are prone to do, I soon settled into the day-to-day routine of the boarding school and geared myself to wait out the next nine months, which often seemed like years. This was one of the sad parts of growing up on an Indian reservation in years gone by.

MY FIRST DAY

My first day at Holy Rosary Mission is one I shall never forget. My parents went to visit the school superintendent while I waited in the back seat of the car. I saw two young boys pulling a red wagon. A larger boy was seated in the wagon. He cracked the air with a large, leather belt and drove the boys like a team of Alaskan huskies.

Later, I would discover that the boy in the wagon was named Omaha. He was riding in the wagon because his feet had been amputated at the ankles. Omaha ran away from Holy Rosary Mission and got caught in one of the year's first blizzards. Tired, cold, and hungry, he found an old abandoned car, climbed in and waited out the storm. When a search party found him the next day, his feet were frozen.

The angry young man in the wagon cracking his belt like a muleskinner was frightening, and, as I would soon find out, for a very good reason. He had discovered that any of the young boys could outrun him for the time being, but as Joe Louis described the boxing master Billy Conn, "He can run, but he can't hide."

It was a foolhardy boy who thought he could taunt Omaha and get away with it. Omaha had a memory like an elephant. If he had to wait days or months to catch up with a boy and mete out punishment, he waited. Long after the perpetrator had forgotten he had crossed Omaha, the boy-man in the red wagon had not.

Inevitably, the time would come when an unsuspecting boy would find himself sprawled on the ground after a crashing punch from Omaha. He was relentless and fearsome, and in this way he recruited the boys to pull

Louis "Omaha" Pretty Bird (in his wagon) escorted by Sister Barbara.

his wagon. Any young boy who refused to provide the service would soon discover this was not a very wise thing to do. Omaha always got his way.

However, these were just some of the things waiting in the wings for me. My immediate concern was what my parents were up to. It seemed they were gone for an awful long time. They had brought me, then removed me and my "Safeway suitcase" (a brown bag) from the car, handed me over to a gentleman named Mr. Burger (who turned out to be a not-so-gentle-man), and climbed back in the car.

My heart sank as I saw my father start the car and head down the road without me. I broke from the grasp of Mr. Burger and started to run after the car. Mr. Burger soon overtook me and gave me a cuff behind the ear. This was my introduction to life at the Indian Mission.

I remember sitting down on the concrete slab in front of the boys' building, called Red Cloud Hall, and crying my heart out. I was frightened and lonely. I thought I would never stop crying.

A young man, obviously a hardened veteran of Mission life, strolled over to me and wordlessly offered me a portion of the honeycomb, dripping with honey, he was munching on. Later, I would find out this was an extremely generous gesture. This boy's name was Gutierrez, and I will always regard him with the greatest respect for his kindness.

Life at the Mission turned out to be one of intermittent loneliness, learning, and growing up. For me, and for thousands of young boys who preceded me, life would never be the same. In the ensuing years, the innocence of childhood would be put to the test.

Like all of the young boys, I found my Mission days to be filled with new friends, the usual scratches and bruises, and in my mind, an excess of unwarranted brutality from the administrators.

No, I never learned to like it. For me, the worse time of the year was when it was time to load up and head back to the Mission for another nine months.

When I hear the youngest of today griping about going back to school, knowing they will be able to return to their homes, to their beds, and above all, to their parents each day after school, that griping seems frivolous to me. But then, each generation has its own cross to bear.

DORMITORY SOUNDS
A heavy ball rolled down the steps
That led from the attic
Above our dorm.
It didn't do it every night,
Just on pitch-black nights
At the midnight hour.
All the boys heard it.

We pulled the covers
Over our heads.
Sometimes the full moon
Would reflect off the snow
And illuminate the ghostly statues
That stood like ominous specters,
Haunting figures
Against the walls
High above our beds.
A tiny nun robed in black,
Without a face,
Floated silently through the aisles.
She never made a sound
And no one ever saw her feet.
The darkness would quake
With a cough or a sneeze
Or someone crying in his sleep.
And we'd pull our covers tight
And pray for the morning sun.

THE BED WETTERS
In a far corner of the dorm,
Segregated from the rest of us,
In their own private hell,
Slept the bed wetters.
Every morning you'd see them
Changing their blankets and sheets.
In their little corner of sadness,
Slept the bed wetters.
They were our friends by day,
But each and every night,
Banished to their darkened corner,
Slept the bed wetters.
Laughing and playing by light,

Dejected and forlorn at night,
Pushed away from sight,
Slept the bed wetters.

QUALITY EDUCATION
It occurred to several of us one day,
I think in Washington, D. C.
As we reminisced about our school days
At the boarding schools and Missions,
That we never talked about Reading,
Writing or Arithmetic,
About Latin, History or Geography,
But we always talked about
The funny things that happened,
The unusual things that happened,
But never about a quality education.

Like Rochester's composition—a classic,
Called "THE SCHOOL PICNIC,"
He substituted "It" for "I"
And here's how it came out:
"It ate so much,
"It got sick,
"It stuck its hand down my throat,
"But It can't!"

Or the new teacher (a priest)
Addresses Joe Pourier (Poor-year),
In a session on the bourgeois.
"My dear Mr. 'Poo-yay,'
Let's discuss the bourgeois."

And poor old Joe
Instantly became
Mr. Poo-yay,
Forget the bourgeois.

PUNISHMENT, NOT EDUCATION

Generations of children were sent to the boarding schools to be indoctrinated. First they were shorn of their hair, clothing, spirituality, customs and traditions—and soon they felt the sting of a leather strap or the slap of an open hand.

They would learn what it is like to be locked in a dark closet as a form of punishment. They would learn how to march to and from all activities. They would all be dressed in chambray shirts and bib overalls so that everyone looked the same. Individualism would become a reason for punishment.

In the late 1960s, things did start to change for the better at the Catholic, Methodist and other religious Indian missions located on the reservations. Everything forbidden to us so many years ago began to be taught—indeed, encouraged. There are now Lakota language instructors and teachers to acquaint the children with the traditions of their ancestors.

But in the old days, speaking Lakota was strictly forbidden; speaking English was mandatory. My mother spoke absolutely no English when she started school at Holy Rosary Mission at Pine Ridge. A former classmate of hers and a good friend, Florence Tibbetts, told me years ago how the older girls would try to protect her from punishment because she was having a difficult time mastering the English language.

Florence, now in her eighties, said, "Your mom used to look for me just shaking with fear. I and my friends always tried to take care of her."

Basil Brave Heart, now a counselor at Little Wound School at Kyle, recalls having to bite down on a large rubber band and having a prefect stretch it to its limits, release it and have it smack viciously against Basil's lips. He was punished thusly for speaking Lakota.

I was a student at Holy Rosary when Mr. John Bryde first came to the Mission as a prefect. He later became a professor at the University of South Dakota. Bryde made it his business to learn the Lakota language, even though the language was forbidden to the Lakota students.

He learned by cornering an elder visiting the Mission and asking him many questions. He would write the English word and the Lakota translation into a small spiral notebook he carried at all times.

Well, John Bryde learned the language all right, but he continued to mete out severe whippings with a leather belt to any boy caught speaking the language he, himself, was trying to learn.

At Holy Rosary, the first week was always the hardest. Many boys and girls would become physically ill with homesickness.

Every night and every morning we were lined up in military ranks for roll call with an older boy acting as our captain. The older boy could be our friend or assailant over the next nine months. Many of the older students acting as captains were extremely cruel to the children under their command. It was not uncommon for an errant boy to be smashed in the face with a fist by the older captains.

At roll call a prefect read off the names of every student while we shouted "present." Anyone not responding was usually on the run. Most of us prayed that the runaways would make it to freedom. Once in a great while they did. But for the most part, they were dragged back to the Indian Mission tired, dirty, hungry and in tears. It was a sad thing to see them captured.

The first captain I recall was a very dark-skinned boy named "Boob." I don't know how he got the name but it certainly fit him. When it came to his cruel treatment of those he commanded, he was, indeed, a boob. For some reason I annoyed him so he directed much of his anger at me. I learned to bite my lip and keep my mouth shut whenever I was under his command.

"Boob" was in command of our march to church in the early morning, our march to the dining room, our behavior at our assigned tables, and our march to Red Cloud Hall after our meals. At any time during these activities, he had the authority to punish his wards. His favorite method was a slap across the face with an open hand or a punch in the stomach or arm with his fist. The rest of the day was under the control of nuns, prefects, brothers and priests.

Every prefect carried a notebook. He entered infractions in the book and the number of infractions was tallied at the end of the week as demerits. If we surpassed our allotted number of demerits for the week, there were penalties. The penalties usually involved barring us from attending the Sunday night movie, one of the pure enjoyments of our days at the Mission school.

On Sunday evenings we would once again stand at roll call while the prefect read the names from a clipboard of those who had accumulated too many demerits. The victims were ordered to step from the ranks and line up against a wall. From there they were sent to bed in the dormitory. The lucky boys often snickered at the losers as they marched off to the gymnasium to see the Sunday movie.

Going back to school was a lonely and traumatic time in our lives. We never knew if there would be new prefects or nuns to teach us or if they would be kind or cruel. We had to leave our homes out on the reservation and the sheltering arms of our parents. We had to leave our pets. We had to leave the good meals our mothers prepared for us and then adjust to the yellow mush and boiled, stringy meat prepared for us by the school cooks. It seems that we were not just lonely, but always hungry.

After all of these years, I still experience the mixed emotions associated with returning to the boarding schools each September. Even the smell of a fall day can bring back those memories.

THE COMFORT OF SOAP AND WATER

We were in our third-floor dormitory in Red Cloud Hall when "Gabby" Brewer came up to us.

"Frosty" Gamette, Tibby Kocer, Basil Brave Heart and I were seated on our U.S. Army-issue bunks and footlockers just chatting away when Gabby approached. He asked, "Do you think my hair will grow out faster if I wash it every night with soap and water?"

We all agreed. "Yeah, sure, sounds like a good plan."

I don't know how Gabby got his nickname. He wasn't that talkative, at least not at the Mission. Maybe he was gabby at home. In all likelihood he probably got his name from one of the Sunday night movies that previewed in the Mission gymnasium every Sunday night. The sidekick of Roy Rogers was Gabby Hayes, if memory serves. But then Gabby Hayes was a short, bewhiskered fellow who in no way resembled our Gabby.

Gabby asked us about the soap and water treatment for his hair because the Jesuit prefects at Holy Rosary had ordered that his head be shaved to the skull. The order was carried out. Gabby's crime? He ran away from the Mission, was caught and returned to the school.

Now let's talk about cruel and unusual punishment. In the spring of that year (in the 1940s) Gabby's father and Gabby's brother Richard went fishing at White Clay Dam on the Pine Ridge Indian Reservation. It must have been over a long holiday weekend. Usually only the students who lived near Holy Rosary made it home for any of the holidays. Pine Ridge Village was only four miles from the Mission.

A tragedy happened. Richard slipped from the bank and fell into the water. Since winter was just now subsiding the water must have been freezing cold. Gabby's father dived into the water in an effort to save his son. Both of them drowned in the frigid water.

My best buddy at the Mission was Gabby's older brother Tommy. I know that Tommy was shattered by the loss of his father and brother. I can't even imagine the hurt that Gabby must have experienced. He was younger and probably more impressionable.

Gabby Brewer was one of those kids you liked immediately. He always had a ready smile and a gentle manner. The Lakota *winyan* (women) would say that they just wanted to *ahniyan* him (squeeze him, like pinching his cheeks).

Gabby would probably have a good laugh to hear this now. He is retirement age. The last time I saw him at Pine Ridge he was talking about putting in for Social Security. He is probably receiving it by now. How the years fly.

After the tragic accident at White Clay dam, Gabby became very quiet. He turned inward. There was no compassion, comforting or counseling by the priests, nuns, brothers or prefects at Holy Rosary. Today, when something tragic happens to school kids, there are counselors to help them understand the tragedy and get through the traumatic experience. There was no such help at the Mission.

Gabby suffered alone and in silence.

Something happened to him. He sneaked away from the Mission one day and headed for his home in Pine Ridge Village. He was captured and returned to the school. He was greeted upon his return with a razor strap and beaten until he had bruises on his legs and buttocks. Such was the compassion of the Jesuit priests.

But that wasn't enough punishment. The next day he was taken to the barbershop and his head was shaved clean. Lakota boys and men take pride in their hair. To shave his head just added insult to injury. But that still wasn't enough punishment, according to the Jesuits.

A sandwich board sign was created and on the sign was written, "I am a runaway." Gabby was forced to wear this sign from morning until bedtime. He even had to wear it to morning Mass, where he could be observed by all of the students, including the girls.

When he came to us and asked, "Do you think my hair will grow out faster if I wash it every night with soap and water?" we wanted it to be true. We hoped with all our hearts that soap and water every night would bring an end to the pain and embarrassment he must have been feeling.

Where do we even begin to categorize the abuse Gabby suffered at a time when he needed counseling, a kind word or an understanding adult to comfort him instead of the beating and humiliation meted out to him?

Gabby had a lot of tough years after he left Holy Rosary Mission. How much of it could have been traced back to the day he was beaten, had his head shaved bald and was further humiliated by having to wear a sign pointing out his supposed transgressions?

But Gabby is one of those Lakota men with a sense of humor and an undying spirit of goodwill. He survived in good fashion and like many of us ex-Mission boys, he survived in spite of all the efforts to make him less of a human being.

I think the soap and water treatment really worked. It seemed that his hair grew in twice as fast as usual. It was only his self-esteem and pride that was stunted for a long time.

HALLOWEENS WERE FUN

Halloween used to be a fun time!

I'm not in the habit of referring to the years I spent at Holy Rosary as "the good old days," but there were without question some good and happy days.

In bygone days, grades one through five were referred to as the "little boys." There was the little boys' gym and the little boys' dormitory. Grades six through eight were one stop above the little boys classification. Grades nine through twelve were the "big boys." I mention these unique classifications because, as we grew from one group to the next, we always lived with the excited anticipation of reaching the next age group plateau. It should go without saying that the low group on the totem pole was the "little boys."

We reached a definite landmark plateau when we moved from the eight grade to the ninth. You see, this meant we left the umbrella of the little boys' dormitory, little boys' tables in the dining hall, and the little boys' seating arrangement at the Sunday night movie.

We became instant "big boys" when we graduated from the eighth grade. We passed through the large French doors that separated the little boys' dorm from the big boys' dorm. We moved far away from the smelly corner in the small boys' dorm where the bedwetters slept. We left the sagging beds with the straw mattresses and moved to the new, Army issue, double-deck bunk beds with our own footlockers.

Even our clothing became grown-up. Left behind were the bib overalls. In their place were blue jeans with, by golly, real belts.

Later, in the military, I heard the expression that pretty well summed up the different age levels at the Mission. Every time one of the enlisted men complained about certain advantages accorded to those of higher rank, the response would be, "Rank has its privileges."

The same situation existed at Holy Rosary. The "big boys" attended dances, had a recreation room and got to go to the once-a-year, big-time Halloween costume party and dance.

The "little boys" got to cut out black cats or color pictures of jack-o'-lanterns in the classroom, but how in the world could this compare to wearing elaborate costumes and going to a big party?

On Sunday night, when the movie was shown in the big boys' gym, little boys got to see the news, cartoons, and the weekly serial, but had to march up to the third floor dormitory (the little boys' dorm) after the serial. Only the big boys got to stay and see the feature movie.

Now this pecking order wasn't restricted to the boys' side of the school. Over on the girls' side the same situation existed. All of the "little girls" couldn't wait to become "high school girls."

This grouping by age covered most aspects of school life. There was the big boys' playground and the little boys' playground. The dining room was divided into groups of big boys and little boys. All of us little boys were assigned a table captained by a big boy.

Even when we lined up in ranks for roll call, our platoons were manned by little boys and the leaders were the big boys. Each day we attended church (which we did seven days a week), the little boys sat in the smaller pews to the front of the church and the big boys sat in the rows to the back of the church.

Several days before Halloween, the little boys knew something was about to happen. The big boys gathered in groups, and we could overhear them laughing and talking about costumes. They would wonder quite casually whether they would be able to recognize their girlfriends in their costumes.

Some of the little boys, the more adventures ones, would gather their friends around them and "accidentally" peek into the big boys' gym and see all of the orange and black decorations, the pictures of witches and black cats, and the carved faces on the jack-o'-lanterns that had transformed the gym into a wonderland.

The one thing most of us missed out on at Halloween was the tricks or treats. Holy Rosary was located out in the country. All of the stories we heard about tricks or treats came to us by the way of books our teachers read to us.

Even today, when I talk to people who lived in communities that allowed them to go out on tricks or treats, I hear their complaints of how times have changed.

They usually say, "You know, back when I was a kid, we never had to worry about finding razor blades or poison in our Halloween candy, there's a bunch of sick people running around these days."

Anyway, when Halloween evening arrived, all of the big boys went off to the "smoking room" or the big boys' dorm to prepare for the big party. The little boys wandered around the gym glancing furtively at the big double door leading from the big boys' dorm, watching and hoping that they would be able to catch a glimpse of their heroes in their Halloween finery. At long last we'd see them coming down the stairs, laughing and joking with each other. We would see pirates, devils, bearded bums and knights. All of us little boys would try to guess the identity of the costumed idols.

Silently we watched as these big boys swashbuckled their way to the Halloween costume party and dance, leaving us to dream about all the good things they were about to experience.

I guess things are going back to the good old days, because I hear and read that the hazards of tricks or treats are causing parents to keep their children at home.

As we watched the big boys head for their party, we would all look at each other and say, "I sure will be glad when I'm a big boy and can go to the Halloween party." Yeah, Halloween sure used to be fun!

BIG BOYS COULD SMOKE

At Holy Rosary, there was a special room set aside for the big boys. Since we were allowed to smoke after we reached the ninth grade, the room was called the "big boys' smoking room," although it was actually our recreation room. Of course, tobacco didn't come soaked in pesticides and herbicides in those days either.

My father, who smoked roll-your-own cigarettes until his fingers were nicotine-stained, lived to the ripe old age of 95. The Bull Durham string hanging from our shirt pockets with the little round label attached was our mark of a grown-up.

Tobacco is a special thing to the Lakota. It is used in prayer bundles. It is used in the *inipi* (sweatlodge) and for all of the Sacred Ceremonies of the Lakota. Our *canupa* (pipe) filled with tobacco is as sacred to the Lakota as the Holy Bible is to the Christian.

But, don't assume that I am promoting cigarettes. I do not smoke and I discourage anyone else from smoking. It is a dirty habit that is also extremely unhealthy. Just visit a hospital patient with emphysema caused by smoking and you will see the damage smoking can do. But that does not diminish the significant way Indians use tobacco in their sacred ceremonies.

WHY WE DIDN'T FREEZE TO DEATH

Out on the Indian reservations, the real challenge is to keep from freezing to death in an area where harsh winter temperatures way below zero are normal. Wood-burning stoves heat homes, along with coal furnaces, electricity and propane gas. When times are difficult and money cannot be found to buy these things, oftentimes families, usually related, move into one house and share the expense of keeping warm.

The bureaucrats in Washington, D.C., in their infinite wisdom, had many houses built on the northern reservations as if they were being constructed for the warm climate of Arizona. The winter winds whistled through like an air conditioner, and if you were not careful you could freeze to death.

The same bureaucrats decided it would be easier to install electric heating, even though many Indian families could not afford the high electricity bills.

When I was growing up at Kyle on the Pine Ridge Reservation, there was a self-sufficiency among the Lakota people that seems miraculous compared to the nearly total dependency of the people living on the reservation today.

When fall was in the air, the people of the tribe got their saws and axes and began to prepare for the winter ahead. There wasn't a home in the Pejuta Haka (Medicine Root District) that did not have one wall covered by wood stacked all the way to the roof.

Later, when I became a student at Holy Rosary Indian Mission, all of the able-bodied boys worked at one time or another helping shovel coal in the basement of the boys' building.

Coal would be dumped down the chutes and several of us would use coal shovels to make room under the chutes for the next truckload.

One day, Lloyd Little Wolf, Frosty Garnette and I were assigned as the coal haulers for the day. The first load of coal had been dumped down the chute, and it was like a mountain extending nearly to the top of the open hatch. The wooden hatch was like a trap door, made of heavy wood and two-by-fours. The three of us climbed to the top of the coal pile and stuck our heads out into the fresh air of a brisk winter day.

Just at that instant, a strong wind caught the hatch and slammed it shut. Since we were standing with our upper bodies well above the ceiling of the coal cellar, the heavy hatch landed on our heads like a pile driver. Little Wolf and I were driven about hip deep into the pile of coal. Fortunately for Frosty Garnette, he was quite a bit shorter than we were, so the heavy lid came to a gentle rest on top of his head without doing any damage. Little Wolf and I saw stars for several minutes and were torn between crying and laughing. I think we did a little of both.

The huge gray cement building known as the boys' building was heated by furnaces in the basement. The dormitories had small steam furnaces that whistled and groaned all night long, but they did an adequate job of keeping us from freezing to death.

The boys' dining room at Holy Rosary was heated by a larger brown fuel-burning furnace. As we trooped into the dining room each morning after church services to a meal of yellow mush and bread, we really appreciated the warmth given off by that old furnace.

If one were big enough and tough enough, he could take his slice of white bread over to the furnace, place it on the grid, and lo and behold, in a few minutes he would have toast. Most of us never got to enjoy this privilege until we reached high school age.

I guess what we learned in those early days in the 1940s and 1950s was self-sufficiency. We were learning that to be ready for the cold winter, we had to think ahead.

If there is any single institution to be blamed for the sad state of affairs on many Indian reservations today, the finger must be pointed at the federal bureaucracy. In an effort to live up to their self-styled role of protector of the Indian people, the government took away the initiative and drive of a once totally self-sufficient people.

Generations of Indians have paid the price for that misplaced paternalism, both on the reservations and in the boarding schools.

SPRING FEVER

By the time the days began to lengthen and the first sprouts of green began to pop up from the earth, the long, hard winter had already begun to take its toll on us. The expression used today is "cabin fever." At Holy Rosary, many of the cold days were spent indoors in the "little boys' gym," so I suppose our affliction, caused by what we perceived to be a never-ending winter, could be called "little boys' gym fever." All winter long, we kept ourselves occupied with games of basketball, indoor baseball (using stuffed socks as a baseball), a homegrown game called "Six and Four Are Ten," making bone horses and wire cowboys, and the usual array of shoot-'em-up cowboys and Indians games.

After an especially exciting movie, our Sunday fare for being good boys, a new round of games began. Movies like *Union Pacific* or *They Died With Their Boots On* brought out the cavalry and Indians. The funny thing was, when we chose sides for combat, it was really hard to find any kids willing to play the part of the cavalry. Everybody wanted to be an Indian.

I recall the sound of turkey gobblers bouncing off every wall, reverberating from pillar to post in the little boys' gym after we saw the movie *Sergeant York*, starring Gary Cooper, one freezing Sunday evening.

But by the time spring began to make its presence felt, most of the boys began to get pretty owly as the "little boys' gym fever" became epidemic. Arguments and fistfights became more frequent and even our guardians, the priests, nuns, brothers and prefects, began to pray for early signs of spring.

Ah, blessed spring, at last! The snow began to melt and the ditches filled with rapidly flowing rivers. It was time to turn the boys loose in this wonderful world of cold water and beautiful mud. Our dormant talents as wood carvers, sailmakers and helmsmen came to the fore as we put our homemade ships to sea on the rapid waters of the ditches and ponds forming in the wake of the melting snow. If you had any talent at all, you had a frigate or a three-masted cargo ship crashing through the rapids of the newly found oceans.

The medicinal value of spring was evident. Our appetites became heartier and our sleep sounder. Our laughter became louder and our play rowdier.

Of course, spring fever was called that for a reason. The days cooped up in a classroom, watching the early buds of spring form on the tree outside the window, heightened the longing to be outdoors.

GABBY

When he first started school
He was a quiet kid with a quick smile.
His older brother Tommy was my pal.
Tommy and I could usually be found
Shooting baskets in the "little boys' gym."

And then we heard how Gabby's and Tommy's father
And their brother drowned at White Clay Dam.
It saddened everyone at the school
To lose a classmate and friend.

Tommy changed a lot, but Gabby ran away.
The priest were real compassionate,
They shaved off all his hair
And made him wear a sign
Tied to his back for all to see.
It read, "I am a runaway."

Gabby got real sick that year.
They said he had "strep throat"
And announced at church one day
That he was very critical and might not live.
So they had a special Mass for him.

Well, Mission boys learn to endure,
And Tommy learned to laugh again.
And things got back to normal once more.
Gabby whipped his illness...
He came back with a full head of hair.

Playing baseball in early spring. Tim Giago can be seen in the front row with his head just above the hands of the boy holding the bat.

SUNDAY NIGHT AT THE MOVIES

Sunday was one of our happiest days,
This was the day of the movies.
What a treat!
This world of the unknown,
This world of the outside,
Of cowboys and Indians,
Horses and automobiles,
Skyscrapers and bridges,
Soldiers and ships,
What a world of fairytales.
We had a ball!

We were all lined up by company each Sunday,
And the black-robed prefect read the rolls,
Ten or more demerits,
James Willard—to the wall,

Peter and Alonzo,
Sioux Boy and Richard Dix,
Ten demerits or more,
Margoose and Jughead,
Louie Boy and Billy Joe,
No movies for you tonight,
To the wall!

NICKNAMES
A Rosebud Sioux once told me
"The Oglala Pine Ridgers really have
Wicked nicknames,"
Wicked in this case meaning
Far out, or wild,
Not bad or terrible,
Unless
You happen to be one of the guys
Tagged with one of the wicked nicknames.

I suppose in later life some of these
Mission names came back
To haunt a man,
To taunt a man.
Not to hurt,
Unless
You happened to be overly sensitive,
Or had been singled out by an ignorant deed.

Each and every name had a story.
Some defied rhyme or reason
And many were pure colloquialism,

Such as Sagué
Or a walking stick,
Which was Lakota for cane.
Nonsense,
Purely nonsensical, for why should a boy
Be named after a walking stick?
There was "The Brown Bomber,"
Not named after the great boxer
But rather after an incident
That actually occurred
One winter night
In the dormitory.
Accident!
It seems the lad took a rather healthy crap
In his bed one night... the evidence was irrefutable.

There was P-2, Dopey and Buck Jones,
Tiny Tim, Rochester and Magpie,
Sioux Boy, Omaha and Duck,
Batman and Curley Bill,
Whiteman, Heavy,
Frosty and Fatty,
Wobbie,
Snazzie, Capone, Dillinger and Plum,
And Mr. Plenty Holes became B. O. Plenty.

We had our private nicknames
For many of the good fathers
And a few nuns.
But of course
We kept these names
A guarded secret.
Because
Father Eagle Beak, Eddie Boy and Fagin

Would tan our hides, like Sister Peakie used to do.
This story was told to me a summer ago
And the teller swears it's true.

All of the guys
Are well known to me
So I am inclined
To believe it.

No way
Could anyone dream up the names,
Or the story behind this narration.
A South Dakota patrolman, it seems,
Stopped a speeding car with four Mission boys,
"Lets have some names," said he.
"Well I'm Jughead,"
"And I'm Bighead,"
"I'm Squashhead," said the third.
"Whoah!"
Screamed the cop, "If you have the nerve to tell me
Your name is Bonehead, I'm running you all in."
"No sir...my name is Spudhead," said the last.

THE ORIGIN OF NICKNAMES

Every Sunday the school gymnasium was turned into a theater. The Catholic priests and nuns selected the movies and tickets were sold at the door to the local reservation townsfolk. Popcorn was ten cents a bag and one could also get a soft drink for a dime. The Church made a small profit from this venture.

Of course, the labor was cheap. Mission boys set up the folding chairs used by the audience and my partner, Chuck "Wobbie" Trimble and I made the popcorn and doubled as counter help. A cruel prefect named John Bryde was our supervisor.

Sunday night became a special night to the Mission boys and girls. Of course, the boys and girls were separated by an entire gym floor. The boys sat on one side of the gym and the girls on the other. In the middle was the paying audience.

When the serial *Zorro* made its debut, every boy had a sword and learned how to slice a "Z" into anything and everything. There were sword fights up and down the stairwells and all over the little boys' gym.

Two brothers, now deceased, picked up their nicknames from the movies. Richard Richards (the last name was pronounced "Rishaw" back then) became Richard Dix after a movie cowboy. His brother, whose first name I do not recall, became "Bozo." Bozo died of a mastoid ear infection when he was still in high school.

I remember walking into the Enlisted Men's Club in Yokosuka, Japan in 1953 and running into Richard Dix. He died several years ago.

Martin White got his nickname "Capone" from a movie, and of course his brother Dennis then became "Dillinger." Western movies seemed to have been the source of several nicknames. A movie cowboy named Buck Jones gave his name to one of the boys. "Dopey Lone Dog" was named after *Snow White and the Seven Dwarfs* came out.

Aloysius Red Elk was tagged as "Rochester," which eventually became plain "Roch," after a Jack Benny movie introduced his sidekick to us. Another Western movie was the source of Bill Irving's name. He became "Curly Bill." Duane Garnette had several nicknames. He was, all at one time, Frosty, Peter Rabbit and Snowshoe. His brother James was "Heavy."

Two Trimble brothers became "Snazzy" and "Fatty" and I'm not so sure they were named for movie characters or movie slang. Of course, there was a boy called "Jughead," and I think he got his name from the Archie comic books. The boys of the Mission started names on their own. Twin brothers Billy and Bobby Brewer were sort of hard to tell apart so the Mission boys named them "Twin." That way they couldn't mistake them. They would just say, "Hey, Twin, come over here."

I've introduced you to Bighead, Squashhead and Spudhead. Of course, Bighead was always called "Bighead," but the other two eventually became "Squash" and "Spud."

There was a Batman, Sioux Boy, Omaha, Duck, Plum, Whiteman, and B.O. Plenty at the Mission school. B.O. came from the Dick Tracy comic book. His real name was Paul Plenty Holes.

We had a boy named Archuleta and I'll only tell you that the last part of the name was "...the Lead Out." And of course, Gutierrez became "Good Arrows."

If you did something unforgettable, it could lead to a nickname, as in the case of "The Brown Bomber," of dormitory accident fame,

Many of the boys had Lakota nicknames. There was Chesli, Sagué, and Yukée, and the only one I will translate is Sagué, which means a cane or walking stick. The other two you will have to look up in a Lakota dictionary because they might gross you out.

I was lucky. I never got a nickname at the Mission. The year I arrived, there was a popular comic book character named "Tiny Tim." But "Tiny Tim" also was the lame boy in Dickens' *A Christmas Carol*, and at the Mission a boy named Leo Wounded Foot already had that nickname. An so even though my name was Tim, I did not get stuck with "Tiny." My last name did go from Giago (pronounced Guy-ay-go) to Guygo. That's about as bad as it got.

There were some pretty neat nicknames on the girls' side of the Mission, but I'll cover that later. But maybe not. I'm still too young to be beat over the head with a frying pan.

Looking back, I realize that I wrote the poem about nicknames fifty years ago.

Richard Dix is dead now. So are Batman, Sioux Boy, Omaha, Whiteman and B.O. Plenty. Dennis "Dillinger" White also died recently.

The twins, Billy and Bobby Brewer, have passed away, as have Curly Bill and Tiny Tim. I went to "Spudhead's" funeral in 2005.

It finally occurred to me that most of the people I've written about in this book are dead.

IN MEMORIAM
SHADOWS FROM THE SPIRIT WORLD

TWO GANGSTERS WHO WERE GOOD GUYS

"Dillinger" died a while back.

Actually, his name was Dennis White and his nickname in the 1940s at Holy Rosary was "Dillinger." He was a classmate of mine.

It was his brother Orville's fault that he got stuck with this nickname.

One Sunday night we all saw a movie about the Mob in Chicago. One of the characters was the notorious mobster Al Capone. One of the wise guys at school (no, not that kind of wise guy) noticed a resemblance between Orville and Al Capone. The next day Orville became "Al Capone."

The name was soon shortened to "Capone," and that is the name he carried from that day on. It followed, of course, that his little brother would be tagged with the nickname "Dillinger."

Dennis's sister Louise fell in love with my cousin Bobby Giago. I searched the obituary for her name but didn't find it. It made me wonder if she is still alive or if she had a nickname also. And I remember his sister Loretta as a great basketball player and cheerleader for the Holy Rosary Crusaders. I saw her name in the obit.

Over the years rumors floated around the reservation that Dennis had been sent to prison and that his brother Orville had met the same fate. Many of us former Mission boys wondered if their nicknames had anything to do with their fate. But, of course, we weren't really sure if any of these rumors held any truth.

I remember Dennis as a fair-haired boy with a quiet and friendly disposition. In a boarding school where one finds some mean-spirited boys and bullies, the more easygoing guys stand out in one's mind. One never forgets the bullies either, but it is the good guys who first come to mind when reminiscing about those bad old boarding school days.

One March the opportunity to build all sorts of kites came about due to the good graces of Mr. Fagan, another prefect destined to become a Jesuit priest. Mr. Fagan got a not-so-nice-nickname from the Mission boys after we saw the movie *Oliver Twist.*

The kite situation comes to mind because, coincidentally, Dennis (Dillinger) constructed a kite patterned after one he had seen in a Sunday night movie. It was a kite built like a square box. He was the envy of all of us when his kite flew longer and higher than any of our crudely constructed kites.

I remember that fabulous kite took a nose-dive into the second floor of Red Cloud Hall, the building that housed our classrooms and dormitories. That was the end of that kite.

When I see an obituary of a friend from the old Mission school, I realize that so many of them have passed on to the Spirit World. I wonder about their lives. What did they do and where did they live? How did they turn out? If there is any truth in the story that Dennis had been in prison, I am glad that he did not die there. I am glad that when his time came he was surrounded by the Lakota friends and relatives who loved him.

Stretch your mind and try to picture some of your classmates from forty or fifty years ago, if you are my age. It is hard to do, but I remember "Dillinger" and his ready smile and contagious laugh.

I hope the road he traveled in this life was not filled with too many bumps and ruts. I hope that the fifty-five grandchildren and forty great-grandchildren he left in this world will always have good memories of him.

I have a photograph taken in the 1940s of the freshman, sophomore, junior and senior classes at Holy Rosary Indian Mission. There, with big smiles on their faces, are Dillinger and Capone.

I hope the spirit of Dennis White makes that journey we are all destined to make, and the road he travels is filled with good memories and happy endings.

WOBBIE

Years have passed,
Or so it seems.
We had scattered to the four corners,
Schoolmates once,
Life-long friends, challenging the world.
The only thing we agreed upon
Was Anchors Aweigh,
Bell bottom trousers, coats of Navy blue,
Notre Dame for me, Army for him,
Johnny Lujack or Doc Blanchard?

We learned to share the delicacies of life,
Kernels of corn
Shucked in tin cans,
Held over an open fire, cooked,
Crispy black, old maids, parched corn.
Popcorn kings of Holy Rosary Mission,
Mr. Bryde's little cooks,
Who took the time to save a little shortening
To spread on our bread
At bun time, fooling Mother Nature.

Boyhood days of camaraderie,
It would surprise both of us
To experience a continuity
Of unending friendship,
Surviving the trials of the years.
This all came about one night.

I sat across the table at
"Top of the Rockies" restaurant,
Watched Wobbie sip a cocktail
In his fine suit and tie.

But I saw a young boy,
Bib overalls, dungaree shirt,
Chapped cheeks and hands,
Laughing as we walked side by side,
Down the Mission road.

PETE CUMMINGS: LIFE WITH A BALL CAP ON BACKWARDS

The obituary accompanying the photo began, "Peter Eugene Cummings, of Porcupine, died Sunday April 18, at the Hot Springs VA Hospital."

Memories of "Pete" came flooding into my mind.

After my father took a job at the Air Force base in Rapid City, we moved there. Fishing and playing games with my Lakota buddies along the banks of the Rapid Creek brought me the acquaintance of the Cummings family. Because all of the kids were tow-headed, it was assumed by some that the Cummings family was "poor white trash." However, they had the blood of the Lakota flowing through their veins.

Yes, the Cummings family was poor, as were most of the Indian families moving to Rapid City during the World War II years looking for work. They came to Rapid City from the Rosebud Reservation.

After playing war games at Rapid Creek, where there was plenty of foliage to hide in, I was often too tired to trudge all the way back to North Rapid to my house on Lemon Avenue, so I would crash with the Cummings boys. This meant we slept six to a bed, three at the head and three at the feet.

When school started in the fall I returned to Holy Rosary Indian Mission on the Pine Ridge Reservation. I was surprised to see four of the Cummings boys show up. There was "Pug," the oldest, Pete, Melvin and Bobby that first year. The smaller boys would start showing up the next year. Pete had been my buddy in Rapid City so we took up where we left off.

The Cummings boys, as I said, had blonde hair. They were immediately labeled as *wasicu* (white) by some of the black-haired Lakota tough guys and challenged to fight. The Lakota boys soon discovered that these Cummings boys knew how to use their fists. After the initial rousting, they were accepted and became a part of the Holy Rosary scenery.

In his obit photo Pete was wearing a ball cap backwards and that sort of explained how he looked at life. His sense of humor was unmatched. He could laugh at himself as easily as he could laugh at others.

The first year he came to the Mission he was about eleven years old. That April, after having endured the first eight months of the school year, Pete and I took a long walk around the Mission grounds and discussed the prospects of running away from the school. That day we started to make plans.

We decided to run away on a Friday afternoon. Many of the kids would be going home for the weekend and we thought we would have a better chance of making it to Rapid City, 120 miles away. Friday was also the day we took our weekly showers and got a fresh set of clothes to wear for the week. We wanted to look our best when we made our break for freedom.

A few days before "the great escape" we took turns sneaking under a fence north of the Mission playgrounds to stash food and other items we thought we would need. We were pretty excited and scared when the chosen Friday arrived. We showered as quickly as we could and made our way to the back of the school dormitory while the other boys were still in the showers. Roll call was still about four hours away, and this would give us a good head start.

We made our getaway, and for the first time in months we felt free. We walked far from any road across the fields toward the community of Oglala. Suddenly we saw a horserider headed our way. We thought about diving in a nearby ditch, but the rider was obviously Lakota and we thought maybe he could help us. We were wrong.

The rider turned out to be a Mr. Brave Heart. His son, Basil, was one of our best friends. Mr. Brave Heart said he felt bad about it, but he had to take us back to the Mission for our own good.

I'll never forget how frightened we were when we rode onto the Mission grounds and saw Father Edwards standing at the entranceway to Red Cloud Hall with a scowl on his face. He took us into his office, took out a leather whip he called "The Cat" and started after Pete first. Pete did not go quietly into the night. Father Edwards had to chase him around the desk several times before catching him, and then he proceeded to beat the daylights out of him with the whip. Pete screamed loud enough to make my hair stand on end.

When Father Edwards grabbed for me, I bit down on my tongue and took the beating of my life without making a sound. He beat me even harder. I remained silent. Well, Pete and I collected enough demerits that day to miss several Sunday night movies.

Pete died of prostate cancer. His brother Bobby, known as "Cotton," died after being struck by an automobile while still a boy and his brother "Pug" died of acute alcoholism while still a young man. His brother Melvin, called "Dutch" at the Mission, served many years on the Oglala Sioux Tribal Council and is currently on the Shannon County School Board. His younger brother Ben, who did not make it to the Mission that first year, owns a credit and loan company in Rapid City.

Pete's obit reads that he was "a humble man who never realized the positive impact he had on all who knew him." As Wakan Tanka (Great Spirit) is my witness, I will attest to that.

THE BROTHERS TWO BEAR
Once upon a time there were Two Bears,
Peter and Alonzo,
They ran away a lot.

The punishment for running away
Was a shaved head.
We never saw Peter or Alonzo
With hair on their heads.
They probably hold the school record
For running away.
But they always got caught
Because they always went in the same directon
And the search party
Went down the road
And waited for them.

Pete Cummings and I talked about
Pete and Alonzo
As we trudged through the fields
To our own freedom.
Mr. Brave Heart tracked us down,
And we knew we couldn't outrun his horse.
He saw the fear in our eyes,
And he was gentle and kind.
He said, "If you were older I would
Help you run, but you could
Never make it now.
I know how you feel.
I also ran away from that place.
You will have to be punished for running away
But I won't let them shave your head
Because you are very small.
But you are very brave."

We saw Peter and Alonzo
Standing by the water fountain.
And we knew we would never laugh at them
Ever again

Because, for a short time,
We had been free.
And we knew what they felt.
But we didn't get our heads shaved.
And we knew that
Peter and Alonzo
Had suffered twice as much as we had.

OMAHA

I was just a little guy when
I first saw him.
Two kids were pulling him
In a big red wagon,
Like a team of horses,
And he cracked a whip
And drove them faster.

"What in the hell are you lookin' at,"
He shouted at me.
As the wagon screeched to a halt,
He took a wild swing.
I darted out of his reach,
To the safety of a flight of stairs
Where he couldn't follow.

I asked my friend, Little Wolf,
About the boy in the wagon
Who was so young and yet so old.
And that was my introduction
To the true story of Omaha.

Omaha in his wagon.

> *He used to be called Louis*
> *Before he ran away.*
>
> *He picked the late fall,*
> *A warm and golden day,*
> *To take his leave*
> *Of the good old Mission,*
> *To head back to the cabin*
> *Far out on the reservation*
> *From which he was taken.*

South Dakota can be strange
At this season of the year,
And the snow fell.
But not an ordinary snow fall.
It was a real, blowing, howling blizzard,
And Louis was out there
In his Mission clothes.

He told the boys later,
When he was released from
The hospital,
Oh, he grew weary and sleepy,
Blinded by the driving snow.
He found an old abandoned car,
Climbed in and went to sleep.

They took him to a faraway city,
A metropolis
Of tall buildings and side streets.
And he told the boys
All the things he had seen
In this wonderful place
By the name of Omaha.

He talked about it endlessly,
Until it became his name.
No one could call him any thing else,
Except the priest at roll call
As he sat in his red wagon
And scowled.

But none of us ever wanted to visit
The town from which Louis got his name.
It frightened us.

Not because of its size,
Not because of its strangeness,
But because this was the city
Where they cut off Omaha's feet.

AGNES GAVE COMPASSION AND STRENGTH TO THE LAKOTA

I lost a good friend recently. The word to describe Agnes Yellow Boy is courageous. Agnes fought a long, hard losing battle to cancer. In the end her smile was weak but it was still there, shining through with a beauty that made it impossible not to return it.

She never had much in the way of material things, but to her friends and family she was a millionaire. There never was a stray child or creature that was allowed to go hungry at her house in Calico on the Pine Ridge Reservation. Even stray news reporters got a warm welcome at her house.

In 1976 I was doing a news broadcast for KEVN-TV in Rapid City. I wanted to show the contrasts in the way Christmas is celebrated on the reservation versus how it is celebrated in the big city. I chose to visit the Yellow Boy family.

Back then her voice was clear and strong. In a short five years she had changed dramatically. This visit she pulled my head down so she could whisper in my ear. Her voice was nearly gone, but even her whisper carried the good will and cheer I had come to know and respect.

The short visit with Agnes and her family on Christmas Eve will be one I will always cherish. She spoke to me about her message to the Lakota people in the Lakota language. She said that things had not been too good for her of late. There had been illness and other tragedies in the family, but she still gave a message of hope and cheer. She expressed her faith in God and said that he would provide.

It was freezing cold that night as I stood in front of her cabin to do my stand-up close on this special Christmas news report. As I looked into the camera and talked about Agnes and about our friendship over the years, I was grateful that the cold wind disguised my tears.

On all of the reservations in this country there are hard-working and honest Indian women such as Agnes. In many ways they are the backbone of the Indian people. They are the mothers who have dedicated their lives to their families and to their people. They are the proud women who have kept alive the traditions and culture of the Lakota nation.

Like Agnes, many knew the loneliness of the boarding schools. Agnes had spent many months away from home, first at the Bureau of Indian Affairs boarding school at Flandreau, South Dakota, and then later at the Holy Rosary Indian Mission, just a stone's throw from her home at Calico.

Because she was a devoted mother she always worried about the conditions on the Pine Ridge Reservation. Whenever I saw her she would inundate me with questions about tribal government and often worried about how the government wasted money. She always talked about what a hard time her children had trying to find work on the reservation. She never slammed anyone, but she always asked about what she could do to make things better.

She always worried about the alcoholism and drugs she saw on the reservation and she was afraid for the future of all the children. She had read about how some children abused their parents and grandparents and she was appalled because such actions were unheard of in her youth.

The lives of many on this huge reservation will be empty because of the loss of this wonderful woman. Her strength, wisdom, wit, compassion and courage have served as a source of inspiration for so many.

Many lives have been made better for having known this Lakota woman. The terrible suffering she must have endured these past few years is over. She now is at rest in the land of her ancestors. She will be missed and I feel sorry for those who never had the opportunity to know her. Her smile and her kindness will always be with me.

Rest in peace my friend. You have earned your place in heaven.

REQUIEMS AND REGRETS

Goldie's gone, hit by a train,
And Bob Cummings by a car.
Many of the Mission kids
Have breathed their last.

The "Prof" who could play a trumpet
Like Doc Severinsen,
Clevie, Big Boy and Tuttle,
Joe Graham and Leon.
Leon by his own hand,
Trying to save himself
From the righteous banter
That numbed his mind
To reality.
Sagué Joe of tuberculosis,
And Clement at Iwo Jima.
The Herman boy in Europe,
Buck Jones in Korea.
Bozo at the BIA hospital.
We helped to dig his grave
Up at the Mission cemetery,
And later, at his funeral,
We listened to shovels of earth
Make a hollow sound
As they crashed upon his casket,
Obliterating the myths,
Awakening our sleeping minds
To reality.

THE GRAVEYARD

"Indian Scout, 7th Cavalry"
Is inscribed on several headstones,
And in one section
Stands the majestic tomb of Red Cloud,
Chief of the Oglala Sioux.
But just to the east of his headstone,
Is a section set aside
And now completely filled
With the graves of the fathers,
The sisters and brothers,
Who traveled here from Europe
And now lie buried
In this graveyard
In the land of the Lakota.
Every graveyard has a spooky tale,
And Holy Rosary Mission graveyard
Is no exception.

One tombstone of red granite
Lies fallen on its face.
It weights about 400 pounds,
And many a priest
Has set it back up,
Only to have it fall again
When a thunderstorm comes over.
On the face of this stone
Is the outline of Satan's face,
Chiseled away periodically
Only to appear again.

Sounds impossible, doesn't it?
But I've seen the stone,
As have hundreds of Mission kids
Before and after me,
And none of us can explain it,
We only accept it.

In graves that are now obscured,
Sunken into the mass of weeds,
Covered by the Dakota sands,
Lost in the vastness of time,
Lie my Grandfather and Grandmother,
And I get an eerie feeling
When I walk the grounds,
And I can almost hear their voices
In the winds that blow
Across these prairie hills.

ANGELS AND DEMONS

SISTER EVIL, WHO WASN'T
To hear us say her name,
You'd think of witches and goblins.
We'd never seen her name in print,
So we said it like it sounded: Sister Evil!!

You see, her name was Sister Ivo,
But we didn't mean any harm,
Because Sister Evil was kind,
She treated our ills, Sister Evil.

There was always some kind of epidemic
That swept over the Mission kids,
Mumps, measles, smallpox,
She was always there to care, Sister Evil.
She spread on the sulfur salve
For our itching bodies,
Pills for our headaches,
Castor oil for our tummies,
Sister Evil.

We didn't mind the "sick room"
Or those little brown pills,
Because she really cared, Sister Evil.

DR. MCNEIL

I'm certain that none of the elderly Lakota ever referred to him except as Dr. McNeil. If they did, I was never around to hear it.

He was a white man who came to the Pine Ridge Reservation, a reservation bordered on one side by Nebraska and on the other side by South Dakota, in the 1930s. He built a house on a high bank overlooking Kyle Dam in the Pejuta Haka (Medicine Root) District in the community of Kyle.

Dr. McNeil had a buckboard drawn by a single horse before he went modern and bought a Ford Model A sedan. He had a makeshift clinic in his house, but most of the time he would climb into the buckboard, his black bag in hand, and head out to the various communities, ranches and farms on the huge reservation visiting his patients, delivering babies and administering to the needs of the elderly. I remember him as a kind man, a general practitioner who often accepted chickens and turkeys for his services.

The fact that the elders trusted him was a major accomplishment in itself. You have to remember that 1930 was only forty years after the dreadful massacre of Lakota men, women and children at Wounded Knee, just about twenty miles up the road from Kyle.

There were many Lakota who vividly remembered that infamous day of December 29, 1890. In fact, as Dr. McNeil made his rounds, he often talked to some of the elders who had been on the very scene of the massacre.

My mother and father had a deep respect for this quiet, unassuming doctor. In fact, the first five children my mother had she had at home on Three Mile Creek. My sister Lillian was the first of her children born in a hospital, followed by me and my little sister Shirley. The older children were delivered with the assistance of a midwife, but I'm sure Dr. McNeil was waiting in the wings.

My father and some of the Lakota elders would tell jokes about Dr. McNeil, but they were jokes filled with affection. Unless the Lakota elders can joke with you or about you, you have not been fully accepted. When they can joke about you, they are comfortable with you and trust you.

My father never tired of telling the story of when Dr. McNeil first arrived at Kyle. Dad said Dr. McNeil was driving his buckboard out of

Kyle one beautiful, bright summer day when he saw a buxom Lakota woman hanging her wet wash on a clothesline. The doctor pulled up the wagon and commented to the woman about the beautiful day. In Lakota she replied, "Lila waste."

Pronounced "Leelah wash tay," the words mean "very good or really good" in Lakota.

Of course the punch line is that Dr. McNeil responded, "Oh, and its Lilly's wash day." The elders would laugh every time Dad told this story, but I think they laughed out of respect for Dr. McNeil and the laughter sort of made him one of their own.

The bank along Potato Creek below Dr. McNeil's house provided great shade on those hot summer days on the reservation. And they were hot! An elderly Lakota man once told me what real heat was all about. He said, "In the old days we used to work in the fields with a team of mules. One day in August it got so hot that the corn in the fields started to pop. Pretty soon the fields were white with popcorn and the mules got confused and nearly went snow blind," he said, chuckling at his own tall tale.

We swam in the dam below the doctor's house and fished there. The water was particularly deep, so that is where the brothers Billy and Johnny Bear, "Dutchie" Apple, and my brother Tony and my sisters could be found. Of course, my cousins, the Gamettes from Potato Creek, spent many summer days there also. We called Potato Creek "Spud Creek."

We used to spend the early morning hours, while it was still cool out, gathering grasshoppers and placing them in a mayonnaise jar. The lid of the jar was punctured with holes so that the grasshoppers could breathe. This was our bait for fishing. My dad clerked at Kieffe's store in Kyle and he was always happy to give us a ball of butcher's twine to use as our fishing lines. We attached the twine to willow tree poles, notched a piece of wood for a floater, attached our hooks to the line and we were ready to catch fish.

The fish were so abundant in the dam that one time my sister Sophie (now deceased) caught two crappies on one hook using a leaf for bait. In those days gone by the dam was graced with the giant birds that nested along its banks, and we would watch them in awe as they waded along the shores and dipped their bills into the water searching for small fish and crawfish.

Quite often Dr. McNeil would appear at the top of the bank and call for a couple of us to come up to his house. We would scamper up that bank like a flash because we knew what was in store. He would hand us a brown bag filled with bottles of ice cold Dr. Pepper. This was long before the invention of pop cans.

To this day I believe a cold pop tastes better in a bottle than in a can.

Perhaps it was because he was a doctor that he always kept "Dr. Pepper" on ice and ready to hand out to the hot and thirsty Indian kids swimming and fishing below his house.

One time we had been at the dam most of the day and we had a stringer of fish, mostly bullheads and sunfish or crappies. Johnny Bear, the adventurous one, wanted to see if the large bullhead we had caught that morning was still alive. He stuck his finger in its mouth and let out an ear-splitting scream as the fish chomped down on that finger.

In pain he jerked his hand into the air and flipped the bullhead about thirty feet on to the bank above us. It landed at the feet of a laughing Dr. McNeil, who had been standing on the bank enjoying the cool breeze coming off the dam and watching us frolic in the water.

I went away to the boarding school at Holy Rosary Mission that fall and seldom saw Dr. McNeil after that. I suspect that I was now too busy doing the things growing boys do to take notice of him as I did when I was little. Years passed and I did my tour in the military and then came home to visit friends and relatives on the Pine Ridge Reservation. I always made it a point to visit the cemetery at Holy Rosary Mission and say a silent prayer at the graves of my grandmother, grandfather, my Aunt Annie and my great-grandmother Lucy Good Shell Woman.

As I walked to that part of the cemetery where the nuns and priests lie buried, I spotted a cross with a familiar name on it. It was the grave of Dr. McNeil.

He had come to the Pine Ridge Reservation as a young man, one who certainly never intended to get rich out here, had become a friend to the

Lakota people and had lived out his life and now lies buried amongst the Indian people he loved.

As I looked at his grave I said to myself, "Lila waste."

ALBERT ROKEY AND MY SISTER

He was a familiar figure to the boys and girls of Holy Rosary Mission. His eyeglasses were as thick as the bottom of a coke bottle and when you looked into his eyes, they appeared to be small and beady, like those of a catfish.

Albert Rokey—I am not sure of the spelling of his name, but that is the way it was pronounced—was the white all-around maintenance man for the Mission boarding school. He had a small house on the campus, and he also had easy access to the little girls at the school.

I do not know how many years he was at the Mission because I was very young when I got there, but many former students remember him because of his eyeglasses. Many of the girls who were between the ages of nine and twelve remember him for other reasons.

Years ago I met with some of them. Because I was a writer and the editor of an Indian newspaper, they wanted to talk to me about what happened to them. One of them was my little sister, Shirley, who is now deceased. Several of the other girls are also now deceased. However, there are a few still alive who will substantiate my comments.

That day in my office they told me a story that horrified me. I know it was true because of the shame and devastation that showed on their faces as they talked. They shared a terrible secret they had kept hidden for more than thirty years.

Shirley had been drinking, probably to get up her courage. "I've kept this inside all these years," she said. "But now I want people to know."

Her story was about Albert Rokey. During the years he was the Mission maintenance man, he enticed young girls to his room with promises of candy and then sexually assaulted them. How many little girls he raped during his tenure at the Mission is unknown. They were too afraid and ashamed to tell anyone.

One day Rokey was no longer at the Mission. Whether he was fired or just moved to another Indian mission is also unknown. Maybe one of the girls did tell. All I know is that he was never punished for his horrible deeds to the little Mission girls.

Most of the girls who were the victims of this demon have suffered greatly. Many never got over the crime committed against them. Some became alcoholics, others became addicted to drugs and some ended their lives as lesbians.

By the time Shirley was fourteen, she was already drinking and getting into fistfights. She liked to show how tough she was, and a lot of the girls were afraid of her. She stayed angry all her life.

It is my contention that the Jesuit priests, Franciscan nuns, and the brothers and prefects of the Mission had the ultimate responsibility for the safety of the boys and girls who boarded nine months out of the year at their school. It was their duty to protect the innocent children from predators and pedophiles. But they didn't.

In fact, I had my own experience with improper touching from a prefect named Mr. Price, who went on to become a priest. It was a terrifying experience I have never fogotten.

I name names here because I want those who believe there was never abuse at the boarding schools to know that the offenders are real, live people. Father Price is now deceased, but then so are many of the boys and girls from Holy Rosary and other Catholic Indian Missions who suffered sexual abuse at the hands of their keepers. They will never be able to point the finger at those who accosted them. They will never get justice.

There were many Albert Rokeys and Mr. Prices at Indian mission boarding schools across America. I still get goosebumps when I meet someone with extremely thick glasses. I know that is unfair, but so too was the sexual abuse Albert Rokey heaped upon the innocent girls at Holy Rosary Mission.

EDDIE BOY AND MAGPIE

Near the end of World War II a Jesuit priest named Father Edwards arrived to become the principal at the Mission school. I was about nine years old at the time, and to many of us about that age he seemed to be a giant of a man. We heard he had been a chaplain in the United States

Army, and he often wore combat boots that stood out beneath his black robe. We were afraid of him.

Many days we would see him attired in hunting gear and carrying his favorite German Mauser rifle as he headed out toward the hills surrounding the Mission school on his way to hunt. Father Edwards had already educated most of us to his limited patience by whipping us mercilessly with a braided leather strap he called "The Cat." We assumed he took the name from the "cat-o'-nine-tails" in the stories about pirates we had read in school.

We learned that when Father Edwards, who had become known as "Eddie Boy" on our list of secret names for some priests and nuns, was about to mete out corporal punishment, he would make all of the students within reach line up to observe. His favorite command of "assume the position" became legendary at HRM. The "position" was one of reaching down and grabbing and holding on to our ankles so he could have better access to our posteriors. And then the flaying with "The Cat" began.

To cry or not to cry soon became the question. We noticed that if one cried loudly enough the whipping would not be so severe. If one maintained the misbegotten stoicism of the Indian male, the beating was prolonged, methodical and harsh. Father Edwards wanted us to show fear and acceptance. He would, by God, get a scream and cry out of us or else. And after the pain and shame, he demanded that we say through our tears, "Thank you Father Edwards."

Many years later Father Edwards' claim to fame would be that he beat more Sioux behinds than any white man in history. I actually heard him say this after he said the opening prayer at a conference of the South Dakota Indian Business Association in 1974. I couldn't believe my ears.

But I suspect the worst damage Father Edwards did ran much deeper. One of the quietest, nicest and friendliest kids at Holy Rosary, when I first met him, was Melvin White Magpie. We called him Magpie and everyone really liked him.

One day all of the boys were lined up in military company ranks in front of Red Cloud Hall. We were standing in line on the dirt road in front of the building.

A wagon with two elderly Lakota women stopped in front of the ranks to speak to the Catholic priest who was about to make roll call. In the back of their horse-drawn buckboard were several cakes and pies, which they'd brought to the Mission to sell to the faculty. I say faculty because we, the students, sure never saw any of these delicacies.

This often happened in those days during World War II when the Lakota needed to make a little money. They often bartered with the priests and nuns at the Mission. They brought pies and cakes, beadwork, star quilts and other foodstuffs and artifacts to sell. The priests and nuns were particularly fond of *wojape*, a Lakota dessert made from wild plums or chokecherries that was sort of like a pudding.

Magpie was standing directly behind the tailgate of the wagon. Within arm's reach was a huge, double-decker, chocolate cake, and he couldn't help himself. He snaked a finger over the edge of the cake and scooped a generous helping of chocolate frosting into his mouth.

Unfortunately for Mr. White Magpie, his childish, dishonest deed was observed by Father Edwards. He stepped quickly to the buckboard, picked up the chocolate cake and smashed it into Magpie's face. Still standing at attention, Magpie licked as much of the cake from his face as he could before he was summoned from the ranks, told to "assume the position" and beaten across the backside with a leather strap.

I believe that even the most unobservant student saw tiny changes in Magpie after that. Although he was always a quiet kid, it seemed he withdrew into himself even more. It wasn't long after this that he was caught doing other things to break the steadfast rules of the Mission.

There used to be a metal culvert that ran from the front of Red Cloud Hall north to the little boys' playgrounds. When the winter snow melted, the culvert drained the water from the front of the building to the ditches at the back. We used this culvert as a tunnel when we played war until the priests decided to put bars across the front of it so we could not climb all the way through.

One day a stray puppy wandered on to the Mission grounds. Several of the older boys immediately took him as a pet and placed him in the culvert. They blocked the south end so he couldn't get out. We didn't know much about different breeds back then, but in remembering, I would say the dog was part beagle. It had sad brown eyes. The poor little mutt had a run-in with a porcupine and still had several quills sticking from his chops. The older boys gently pulled the quills while they fed the hungry dog scraps they had slipped into their pockets from the dining hall that day.

Of course, a secret such as a pet dog could not be kept a secret for long. Father Edwards spotted the dog peeking through the bars of the culvert. He called all of the boys together and then he went to his office and returned with his favorite hunting rifle, the German Mauser.

Father Edwards admonished us for breaking the rules and told us we had to be punished. During this harangue we could hear the dog whimpering at the bars of the culvert. He bolted a round of ammo into the chamber of his rifle and with great ceremony strode to the end of the culvert, aimed and fired one round into the forehead of the little dog. The last sound the puppy made was a mournful yelp.

I was standing beside Magpie, and the thing I remember the most is that Magpie's hands and head started to shake as he fought back the tears. The rest of us were too shocked to do anything except stare in disbelief, tears welling up in many eyes.

Father Edwards snorted, ejected the shell casing from the rifle, picked it up and put it into the pocket on his black robe and headed back to his office. We all stood around dumbfounded, still sniffing the scent of burning gunpowder with the report of the rifle ringing in our ears.

Melvin White Magpie died, many years later, in the state prison in Lincoln, Nebraska. I have never asked why he was sent there.

Perhaps what happened at Holy Rosary contributed to whatever caused him to end up behind bars. I don't know. I suppose there could be a thousand reasons. Then again, no one will ever know why a gentle and kind boy turns into a criminal. So many of my Mission buddies did. And so many are dead now, some by their own hand and others of the diseases caused by alcohol and drugs.

I will always remember Melvin White Magpie licking furiously at the chocolate icing on his face. And I will remember him fighting back the tears as his pet dog died. I will never picture him as a hardened criminal wasting his life behind the bars of the prison in Nebraska. To me he will always be that quiet and gentle friend we called Magpie.

A few months after Father Edwards shot the puppy, we broke the rules again. This time it was a kitten. It was small, gray and very hungry. This time we hid the animal in the outhouse located on the little boys' playground. All of the boys knew the cat was hidden there and used the outhouse with great caution so the kitten would not escape. We sneaked food from the dining hall and for about two weeks the kitten lived a good life with plenty of food and plenty of hands to pet it.

Once again it was in the early morning when the command was given for us to line up in company ranks near the outhouse. We all had lumps in our throats because we knew the kitten had been discovered.

Father Edwards cautiously opened the outhouse door and extracted the kitten. In fear it scratched his hand, causing him to let out a loud "ouch" and causing a fearful titter to go through the ranks.

With theatrical flair, Father Edwards held the kitten in the air and asked, "Now what do you think we should do with this little piece of contraband?" We knew he wasn't waiting for an answer from us so we remained silent.

Father Edwards (Eddie Boy) stands amidst Indian students at Holy Rosary Mission.

Without further ado, Eddie Boy took the cat by the tail, spun it around his head several times and then crashed its head into a tree. The kitten reacted convulsively and died.

We were boys who had not even reached our teens. Now what possible lesson had we learned from this display of absolute cruelty? Aside from developing an intense hatred for Father Edwards, I think most of us came away with the lesson that never in our lifetimes would we ever be cruel to defenseless animals.

For me the lesson has been one I have carried all of my life.

EDDIE BOY

He was an ex-Army chaplain,
And the first day he greeted us,
He lined us up in company columns,
And flexed his muscular shoulders
As he paraded to and fro,
Still clad
In his Army fatigues.
If he was trying to scare us,
He sure succeeded that first day.
'Cause he waved a braided whip
Before our nervous noses,
And formally introduced us to this singular weapon.
"The Cat"
Was the name we remembered it by.

"Assume the position" became a by-word,
As we bent over and grabbed our ankles.
"I shall chastise your posteriors,"
Was his battle cry.
And a new reign of terror began.
"The Cat"
Brought fear to the hearts of us all.
We had always been survivors,
And yet, we were afraid
Of this giant in the long black robe
Who intimidated us.
With a permanent scowl on his face,
He struck,
And sent us scurrying to our beds.

Little guys can adjust to anything
And we adjusted to Eddie Boy,
Until one day we found a little kitten.

We hid it in the outhouse,
And snuck it food from the kitchen.
Poor cat,
Eddie Boy discovered it one day.

"Form company columns," he snarled,
And he held the kitten up for all to see.
But he wouldn't hurt it, would he?
He's a Catholic Priest, Society of Jesus,
Dear God!
He smashed its head against a tree.

We buried that little grey kitten,
And even the tough guys cried.
As we erected a tiny cross,
We wondered why we prayed.
Oh God! We wept in our secret hearts,
How could a priest be so cruel?

YOUNG LOVE — AND LOSS

MISSION BOYS AND MISSION GIRLS
Sunday afternoons at the picnic grounds,
We got to see our girlfriends.
Shyly, we'd stroll together,
Shyly, touching hands.
But always watching for the nuns,
Who would chide our boldness,
With a click of their tongues.
The altar boys really had it made,
And all those tortured hours,
Memorizing our prayers in Latin,
Racking our minds while the others played.
It all paid off at Communion time,
As we held the golden tray
Beneath our girlfriend's chin.

The girls took their afternoon walk,
Down the dirt road by the boys' dorm.
And we always found excuses,
To be standing near the road,
Throwing a baseball back and forth,
Hoping to catch our girl's eye
As she walked demurely by!

We had our secret mail train
That delivered twice a week.
And we'd write our love notes scrupulously,
Discreetly pass them to the laundry girls,
As they delivered the clean clothes,
And returned with baskets to the girls' dorm,
After delivering our mail and picking up theirs.

Even at the movies on Sunday night,
We were segregated by the priest,
And could only watch across the gym floor,
Our girlfriends on the other side.
We felt the pains of youthful love,
The emptiness of separation,
But we were never told why.
Why was it wrong for us to love?
To want to be together?
Instead of natural feeling
An Indian boy felt for an Indian girl,
With all of the emotions
A Lakota heart could suffer.
The scars that came were deep,
Many of us never recovered
From the trauma of growing up
With a rope around our necks,
Ignorant of the emotion caused by love,
Yet trying to fulfill a deep commitment
We never really understood.

AN OLD PHOTOGRAPH BRINGS BACK MEMORIES

The photograph was standard. It was maybe three-by-five inches in size. But, back in those days the photos only came in black and white.

They always had a glossy finish and you did not want to put your fingers on that finish for fear of destroying the picture.

The photo was of the Holy Rosary Indian Mission girls' high school class. High school back then included grades nine through twelve. So this particular photo was of the graduating classes of 1952 through 1955.

A Jesuit priest named Father Zimmerman was famous across the Pine Ridge and Rosebud reservations for the photos he took. He would visit a community, get family members together and take their picture. It would be safe to say that the photos of Father Zimmerman, if pulled together into a collection, would give a good photo history of these two reservations from the 1930s up to the 1950s.

I suppose most of these photographs are archived at the Jesuit school at Marquette University. This is the place where many of the school records from the Indian missions ended up. Of course, most of my personal school records were conveniently lost when I started writing about the abuses and the horror experienced by many Lakota children at the Indian missions. If you can't kill the messenger, make him disappear.

The photo of the high school girls was taken by Father Zimmerman. He was one of the kindest priests I have ever met. For some reason unbeknownst to the high school boys, Father Zimmerman made extra copies of that photo and passed them out to us. I believe he knew that most of us had girlfriends over on the girls' side of the Mission, and he rewarded us for our good behavior by giving us photos of the entire class.

The scissors came out and each of us cut out the photo of the one for whom we had set our cap. By the time the face of our loved one was cut from the photo, the pictures were pretty small. However, we tucked them away in our wallets, at least those of us who had wallets. Now the only thing our wallets lacked was money. There was no such thing as credit cards or Blockbuster video cards back then.

It is surprising to me how many of my former schoolmates remember the time Father Zimmerman gave us that photo. Many of us carried our own cut-out photo until it became cracked and yellow with age.

I ran across that photo of the entire class of Lakota high school girls recently, and I immediately focused on the face of the girl who had caught my fancy when I was in high school. She was as beautiful as I remembered, and my thoughts went back to the day Father Zimmerman gave us that picture.

There were some good priests, nuns and brothers at Holy Rosary Indian Mission, and although I write about the bad apples at times, I cannot forget those who were kind and considerate. Just as the scandal in the Catholic Church is spreading across America, I realize there are many devoted priests and nuns who never abused children and who really believed in the mission that brought them to Indian Country.

And now that I have a copy of the photo given to us many years ago by Father Zimmerman, I realize that he knew quite a lot about love and about the dreams of the young Indian boys at the Mission.

THE SODALITY DANCE

"You're dancing much too closely,"
The good nun said so sweetly.
"And if you do not push apart
I'll crack your head completely."
We stood across the gym and eyed
The lovely, comely lasses,
And shyly tried to shift our gaze
From all those lovely asses.
So seldom did we see the girls,
Their presence made us nervous,
Like Guam and Johnson Island did
When I was in the service.

We really weren't such rotten guys,
Our thoughts we did keep pure,
'Cause if we always thought bad thoughts,
We'd lose our minds for sure.
Our catechism taught us this.
Lord knows we did our best.
The girls that made us horny

Were just the Devil's test.
Our monthly dances were great fun,
A time of trial and error.
The lovely girls did their part
To overcome our terror.
"Put Another Nickel In,"
Teresa sang so sweetly,
As she floated in my arms,
I held her so discreetly.
White man's dances could be strange,
Unlike an Indian pow-wow.
"Here comes an angry-looking nun
Afraid I'll have to run now."

"ROMANCE," HRM-STYLE

Watching *My Fair Lady* for the tenth time and relishing this, my favorite musical play, I had my memory jogged by the preparations made by Eliza Doolittle, Professor Henry Higgins and Colonel Pickering for the grand ball. It reminded me of those exciting evenings we donned our Sunday finery as we prepared for the sodality dances held in the high school gymnasium.

Webster's New Collegiate Dictionary defines sodality as "brotherhood, community, or organized society or fellowship, or a devotional or charitable association of Roman Catholic laity." You would assume that our "social club" encompassed all three definitions,

Back in the 1950s the boys and girls were completely segregated at Holy Rosary. Only on Sundays, when we gathered together at the Mission picnic grounds, were we allowed mingling, but under close supervision. To hold a girl's hand invited a reprimand from the nuns, scholastics and priests who were our mentors.

Needless to say, we had our secret way of communicating our adolescent feelings of love to the objects of our affections. The most popular way was to use the "laundry room express." Once a week the high school girls would bring baskets of freshly done laundry to the boys' side. The clean clothes were delivered to the second floor of the Red Cloud Building, which housed our classrooms and dormitories. Quite discreetly the older boys would help the girls unload the laundry from the baskets and the girls would slip them letters from their girlfriends on the other side.

At the same time, the boys would slip letters to the girls before they headed back to their side with their empty baskets. This was the Mission secret mail delivery and receiving system. It worked for all of the years I was a student there, and, as far as I know, it was never discovered by the usually alert nuns and Jesuits.

After the mail was delivered we would slip off to a quiet place where we would not be observed and read our love letters. We would immediately write responses and wait for the next laundry delivery day.

Is it any wonder that the sodality dances and the anticipation of holding the girl of your dreams in your arms, even if it was supervised and at arm's length, worked the boys up into a lather? Why, it was almost enough to cause cardiac arrest in a yak!

All of us high school boys knew this was a special day. We had to be certain to make it to the laundry room to pick up our Sunday suits and ties before the day was out. If we could find a few spare moments between the drudgery of classroom work and our school job, we rushed up to the dormitory on the third floor of Red Cloud Hall and put a quick spit shine on our Sunday shoes.

I served as the school's barber, and I knew that this would be one of my busiest days. The high-school-age boys lined up at my shop, located in the shower room. Never did I receive so many firm instructions about their hair cutting as on sodality dance day.

The footlockers came out from beneath our bunks, where we kept our containers of red Teel liquid toothpaste, safety razors and exotic shaving lotions. Although most of us hadn't even started a growth of peach fuzz yet, we lathered up and hacked away at our tender faces until they glistened.

We splashed on a little "foo-foo juice," which made most of us smell like French street walkers, tried to put the most debonair of knots in our flashy neckties, slicked our hair down with a few gobs of Brilliantine hair oil, checked ourselves over in the smoky mirrors one last time, smiled bravely at each other and set out on our great adventure.

The band struck up the first dance, and most of us lined the walls like proverbial wall flowers, frightened to death of making the first move. With our hearts beating wildly in our chests, we finally made the long walk across the gym floor to seek out the girls of our dreams.

I remember a few of the members of the dance band. There, with his trumpet pressed to his lips, was Bob "Professor" Clifford. On the sax was Billy Bear, and tapping lightly on the drums was Chuck "Wobbie" Trimble.

We moved about the dance floor with all of the fluidity of department store mannequins, and as our fear subsided, we even became so bold as to throw in a trick step or two.

The lights in the gym were kept pretty low, but the Jesuit priests and the nuns circled the dance floor like coyotes around a campfire. You could almost see their eyes glowing in the dark. If we happened to get a bit too close while dancing, one would immediately descend upon us, push us apart and give us a warning. Two warnings and our evening ended abruptly. I blame this for the fact that I never learned to dance well. Too many interruptions.

The band ventured "Rag Mop" and "Put Another Nickel In — In the Nickelodeon," and they sounded like all the big bands of the era to us.

Life at the Indian Mission did have its moments. Like the song in *My Fair Lady*, "I could have danced all night!"

X-RATED BOOKS
My sisters, who lived on the girls' side,
Told us that **True Confessions** *was taboo.*
The nuns would have a fit
If they caught any Mission girls
Reading and savoring "the Devil's pulp."

Of course we never read that sissy stuff,
So we were glad to see the nuns ban it.
But boy, we sure did read comic books,
Batman, Captain America, Captain Marvel,
The Plastic Man, The Green Hornet *and* **Superman***!*
By the time we got done, the color was gone.
They changed hands so many times it rubbed off,
And it seemed we had to wait forever
For that comic book to reach our sticky hands.
But when it did, we read it forty times!

One time, Frosty, Heavy, Little Wolf and I,
Were concentrating on a new comic book.
There was this powerful lady called "Wonder Woman,"
And we all crowded around saying "turn the page!"
When we heard a familiar cough.
"Eddie Boy" sneaked up on us,
And snatched that comic book from our hands.

He studied the book with his familiar scowl,
And glanced menacingly
In our direction from time to time,
He rolled the book up and glowered at us.
"This book is an evil, nasty, filthy book!
"It will poison your young innocent minds!
"She is a half-naked creature of the Devil!
"Assume the position! (grab your ankles)
"I shall severely chastise your posteriors!"

Well, we sure took a mean licking that time,
And we really learned a valuable lesson.
Whenever we got another **Wonder Woman** *comic book*
We posted guards in all directions,
And examined that book with a fine-tooth comb.

HUNGER
BODY AND SOUL

AN APPLE A DAY

When you reached the ninth grade,
You were considered a "big guy,"
And you got a lot of special privileges,
Such as apple picking time.

Buffalo Gap seemed like a thousand miles away,
And we all climbed into the open trucks,
Really looking forward to this work detail
Called apple picking time.

It was early fall and the Paha Sapa,
The sacred Black Hills, drew nearer,
As we peered through the bars on the cattle truck,
Looking forward to apple picking time.

Most of us were plenty damned sick by lunch time,
From all those apples we'd devoured,
But boy, they were juicy and good,
That first day,
At apple picking time.

We always got a special treat for lunch,
On these long work details,

Peanut butter and syrup sandwiches,
Added to the joy
Of apple picking time.

The Mission's just around the bend,
Our lookout whispered as the truck headed home
And we pitched the gunny sacks in the ditch,
Our special cache,
At apple picking time.

On those long cold Dakota winter days,
We used to remember the apple fights,
And we wondered why we were so wasteful,
As our stomachs growled
After apple picking time.

But we never learned a thing,
And every year we had a feast,
And we threw apples at anything that moved,
'Cause there'll always be another
Apple picking time.

BUN TIME

At three o'clock the bell would chime,
We all were well conditioned.
Like Pavlov's dogs we knew the time,
The chime was quite sufficient.

It didn't matter where we played,
The distance we could cover.
We only knew that if we strayed

Too long that we'd discover
The buns were long gone when we arrived.

The older boys would snicker,
Because they always realized
It did no good to bicker.

The fathers stood with hidden grins,
We choked on hungry tears.
They chided us for all our sins,
And prayed that the coming years

Would chasten us and make us good,
They prayed for our salvation.
So next, when bun time rolled around,
We would not face starvation.

If only we would be on time,
The buns would feed so many.
To take the lead and stand in line?
It didn't cost a penny.

I learned my lesson good and sound,
I joined the baker's trade.
And now when bun time rolls around
I eat the buns I've made.

CHICKEN IN A SHOVEL

Hell, what's so special about "Chicken-in-a-Basket?"
Have you ever tried "Chicken-in-a-Shovel?" We did,
And here's how it happened.

As I told you before,
We were always so damned hungry.
The watery soup we usually got,
Didn't do much to fill a growing boy.
And besides,
We used to get awfully tired of boiled everything.
Boiled potatoes, boiled meat,
Boiled cabbage, boiled carrots, boiled mush,
And just 'bout anything that fit in a kettle!

We always heard rumors about mice,
And when the boiled soup was poured,
We'd check our bowls,
Looking for a mouse, or a part of a mouse,
That was supposed to be meat,
That added flavor to the soup.
Of course, we really believed this!
And we still aren't sure we were wrong!

Well, Wobbie, Frosty, and I were walking,
It was a warm Saturday afternoon,
Not a prefect in sight,
Just a perfect view of the chicken yard.
And somehow, this fat little hen got loose,
So we gallantly decided to rescue it,
And take it on a long walk with us
Out of sight in the Mission hills.
As we strolled along, we decided to draw straws,
'Cause none of us wanted to kill that poor bird.
And Frosty lost, and wrung that chicken's neck,
But we weren't ready to feast yet.
How in the hell do you prepare a chicken?
And then,
What the hell do you cook it in?

Well, Wobbie solved that problem by finding a shovel,
And Frosty saved the day by finding a match.

That bird was the color of coal
When we got done burning it in the shovel,
But Frosty, Wobbie and I just sat by the fire,
Feeling like Robin Hood and his merry men.
We chowed down on that blackened bird,
And even the Kentucky Colonel couldn't top that feast,
Because KOOL-EE-AH!
We pulled off a good one on the Mission!

RAW POTATO SYNDROME

We worked like a team,
One would drag the gunny sack,
And the other would shovel in the spuds.
On a real good day,
We could earn as much
As a quarter apiece.

That wasn't too bad for a ten-hour day,
Because when you're ten years old,
A quarter goes a long way.
Of course you didn't get cash,
Just credits to your account
At the Mission candy store.

We were always so damned hungry,
We'd eat just about anything,
If it didn't eat us first,
And raw potatoes made the menu.

With a dash of salt,
They really weren't that bad!

Boy, did we pay the price that night,
The dorm smelled like a live skunk
Had been turned loose on us.
And the still of the night,
Was shattered by gas leaks
That brought boos and laughter.

But as nasty as we were,
After our spud picking trips,
A saintly nun gassed us all!

Right there in study hall,
Sister Peakie put us to shame
With a "high C" we still remember with awe.

It was reading time, not a sound to be heard,
The classroom as quiet as a morgue,
Except for the ruffling of pages turning,
When from the front of the class,
From behind Sister Peakie's desk,
Came a screeching roar that stunned us all!!

Our eyes were riveted on her now,
And tiny beads of perspiration formed on her lips
As eighty pairs of eyes stared transfixed,
In disbelief that a nun could fart!
The sanctity of our thoughts smashed
By this bewildering revelation.

But Sister Peakie saved the day.
She began making loud noises

As she nervously spat upon her thumb,
Trying to moisten it to turn a page.
She fled from the room with a bright red face,
As we rolled in the aisles with laughter.
But strangely enough for us,
Sister Peakie seemed more human after that.

And some of us even began to like her,
Because we knew one thing for sure,
If we were ever to invite her to compete
In a farting contest,
She'd beat us by a mile—every time.

PLEASANT CHORES
Anything to do with food,
These were pleasant chores,
Duty in the bakery,
The smell of fresh bread.
Biting into warm buns,
Life at the Mission became livable.

Mondays we lined up for roll call,
And anticipated the call
For sweepers in the gym.
Sweeping up popcorn
From the Sunday night movie,
Life at the Mission became livable.

We'd get the huge push brooms,
Sweep the popcorn into piles,
And sometimes find a sack

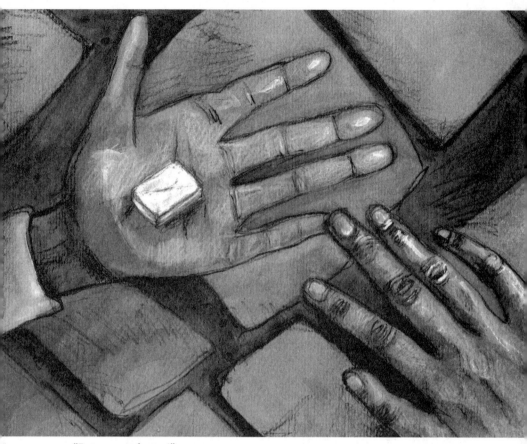

"Bet you one butter!"

With a few kernels intact,
Pick the good kernels out,
Life at the Mission became livable.

Our pals would be waiting,
As we returned from the gym
With sacks of popcorn
Sorted from the sweepings,
Well dusted and edible, we shared,
And life at the Mission became livable.

BET YOU ONE BUTTER

One tiny cube per meal,
Legal tender.
Want a favor?
Cost you two butters.
Make a bet?
Butters for one week.
If you got caught,
Cost you ten demerits.

Hell, some kids
Never tasted butter for a year,
But we bartered,
We bet.
We paid our debts,
With those tiny cubes,
Legal tender,
Mission money!

THE GARDEN

Everybody loved Brother Schlienger.
He was called "Slinger" by most of us,
And he had a green, green thumb.
His garden was the Mission's delight.

We all remember cabbage, carrots, watermelons,
Onions, turnips, tomatoes and cucumbers,
Grown with love in "Slinger's garden"!
A temptation to the most righteous.

Every time I eat a raw cabbage,
Even today, I think of "Slinger"
And the stolen treasures we shared,
From Brother "Slinger's" garden.

THE DINING ROOM

In the center of the long table,
Flanked by long wooden benches,
A solitary tray stood,
Stacked high with bread.

"Bless us, O Lord, for these Thy gifts,"
(We edge toward the bread)
"Which we are about to receive,"
(Our hands flex nervously
As we eyeball the tray of bread)

"Through Thy bounty,"
KrrrrrrTmmp!!!
At least I got a half-slice.
But someday
I'm going to learn
The rest of that prayer
Besides the beginning
And "Amen."

SHARDS OF MEMORY
WHAT CUTS INTO MEMORY IS CARRIED
IN THE BLOOD FOREVER . . .

SHADOWS OF WORLD WAR I

First the Army bunks arrived,
Double deckers.
Real mattresses,
Not like the old ones
That were stuffed with corn shucks,
And Lordy—we were given genuine footlockers.

We couldn't believe our good fortune.
And we worked long
And we worked hard,
Putting those fine bunks together.

And when we were done,
We looked with pride upon our new barracks.
A few days later a truck stopped,
Cardboard boxes,
Stacked five high,
Loaded on the back like in the movies.
We all gathered and milled around,
What other gifts were in store for us?

Father "Eddie Boy" lined us up.
"Eyes right! Straighten those ranks!"

He boomed in his paratrooper's voice,
And we toed the line.

Our eyes never leaving those cardboard boxes,
The palms of our hands itchy and sweaty.
Eddie Boy was just like Hamlet on stage.
He strode with black robes flowing
And pulled a box from the truck.

He paused with a smile on his face, then
Letting it all sink in,
He ripped the lid from the box.

There before our very eyes was World War I,
Tan uniforms with high snap collars,
Brass buttons that shone.
Yards and yards of leggings.
Just like Gary Cooper wore
In the movie Sergeant York!

Some of the little guys had a hard time
Finding some small enough.
But "Buddy Ace" took charge
(Years later he made the cover of Life
As a Green Beret)
And began to issue uniforms.

For weeks we were kept busy,
Scrounging up laundry ink
To color insignias on our uniforms.

Suddenly we were not just "Mission Boys."
We were Sergeants, Corporals, Privates and others,
As all of the ranks appeared.

And when all the preparations were done,
World War I, Custer's Last Stand
World War II, and the Civil War began!

General Buddy Ace marched us to war,
In perfect step we marched
As imaginary shells burst around us.

Years later, in Pusan, Korea,
I marched along in the bitter cold,
And a smile crossed my face,
As I thought of those war games,
We played with such intensity,
And the warmth of those thoughts made it easier.

HOT SHOWERS AND KEROSENE
Friday was always shower day.
Little guys first, big guys last,
A clean set of clothes
To last a whole week,
Until the next shower day.

And I guess we smelled pretty ripe,
After seven showerless days,
But you know, we never really noticed,
I think because the kerosene smelled worse.

But after a few years,
Somebody, probably the coach,
Thought up a way to make it smell better,
By adding some real hair oil to it.

Girls enjoying recess at Red Cloud Hall, Holy Rosary Mission, about 1945.

It sweetened the smell a little,
And improved our grooming habits,
But you know, the girls never really noticed.

You see, shower day we were deloused,
And kerosene in the hair
Was the major weapon
That killed all the cooties on our heads.

And with a little hair oil added,
We slicked down our hair
And groomed ourselves like peacocks,
Trying to impress the girls.
But you know, they never really noticed.

Shower days,
A fine-tooth comb,
Kerosene,
Deloused,
Delighted,
Deserted

By our lovely girlfriends,
Until the kerosene wore off.

THE MISSION BAND
Whiteyes played the trumpet.
He was just a growing boy,
And he looked awkward
With his crewcut
And his long blue cape,
His hat sat down on his ears.

That was the year Crazy Thunder
Was our band teacher.
Wobbie never played the drums better,
Nor Duck and I our trumpets,
But then Crazy Thunder was like
One of us.

He made us laugh, and the band
Was fun.
We still remember the old German.
He threw erasers at us when
We hit a sour note,
Or smacked a long ruler
Across our hands and heads
For carrying on and laughing.
But Crazy Thunder wasn't that way.

Our crowning glory came one Sunday afternoon,
Just before the basketball game.
We looked like troopers in our uniforms,

The Mission Band. Tim Giago is in the front row, second from the left (with trumpet).

And we struck up a Sousa march
That rumbled and rumbled against
The walls and windows of the gym.
We could hear the girls coming
From the girls' side of the school.
We puffed out our chests as they
Oooh'd and aah'd.

Likely they remembered our shame
When we had the St. Francis band
Play for us one day.
They sounded like professionals
While we sounded like first graders.
But that was before Crazy Thunder
Taught us how to play.

THE RADIO
It had been dropped so many times,
You could see the tubes
Glowing orange
Through the busted case.

The knobs were missing
And the selector was guesswork.
Ninth-graders on up,
The big boys
Were the privileged few
Who could listen to the radio,
Savor the music,
And hear the news.

When the state tournament rolled around,
We gathered around
That busted brown box,
And listened intently
To every single play.
We cheered on the Crusaders
Of good ole Holy Rosary Mission.

Yeah, Cuny and Joe Hawk,
Hooray Red Wolf, and Bozo,
Get'em Richard Dix.
Kill'em Sioux Boy,
Union Coach Clifford!

It's Notre Dame of Sioux Falls
And the Crusaders of Holy Rosary Mission,
In the State Championship finals.

We crowd the radio
And things are real tense.
The lead changes hands,
Over and over.
It's Red Wolf, and John Siers,
Scoring point after point.
Red Wolf and Herb Colhoff

The Holy Rosary Mission basketball team in 1949. From left to right: Chris Red Wolf, "Bozo" Richards, Coach Bob Clifford, Herb Colhoff, "Mouse" Morgan, Black Feather.

Start a methodical stall,
Rosary 38, Notre Dame 36!

The radio's still blaring away,
We're jumping up and down,
Shaking hands
And cheering wildly,
Two years in a row,
The state championship.
And then,
There's silence.
The broken down radio plays on...

Congratulations to the Indian boys,
"From Holy Rosary Mission...
"They played a great game..."

THE COACH

I was in a city far from the Mission,
And I read in the newspaper
That the coach had died,
An old man
Struck down by a car
As he walked along the road.

He was always there at the Mission
From my earliest recollection.
And the older boys,
They remembered
That he was there before them.

But then he was a young man.
The gold in his teeth twinkled
Whenever he smiled,
And he was kind and gentle.
I never saw him angry,
Except to defend a boy
Struck by an angry priest.

But even then he did it with dignity,
And made the priest feel guilty,
Because the coach was an Indian
like us.

But back then we never knew
Why he meant so much to us.
The trophies still stand
Behind glass doors, shining—
The State Championship
We earned for the Coach
Against the all-white school.

But he's gone now,
Buried at the Mission he loved,
Forgotten by the boys
Who have traveled far,
Unknown by the young ones
Who will never know
What they missed.

RAH! BLUE AND WHITE!

We trotted onto the football field,
Gazed apprehensively at the opposition,
Clad in their green and gold,
Solid plastic helmets with facemasks,
The Irish of Cathedral High.
And then we looked at each other,
The Crusaders of Holy Rosary Mission,
Hand-me-down uniforms,
Of various hues and colors,
As our cheering section sang,
"Rah! Blue and White!"

Helmets made of soft leather,
Like gloves with holes for the ears,
You could fold up and put into your pocket.
Canvas pants and high top shoes,
Spectacles from the '20s,
Like Red Grange and the boys.

The Irish of Cathedral High,
Snickered and mocked our old fashions
But this soon became respect.
Laughter turned to admiration,
Cockiness to surprise, when
Once the whistle blew.

FIGHT

"Heyupo!"
Fight, Fight, Fight!
And we'd drop whatever we were doing,
Run like hell in the direction of the call,
Form a big circle around the combatants,
And cheer them on in the fray.

If one got knocked into the crowd,
He was seized by many hands,
And shoved head first at his opponent,
The fight would go on while we cheered,
And waited for the victor to drop the foe.

We all know what it was like
To be smack in the middle of the circle,
'Cuz you weren't a Mission boy
Until you'd been challenged and tested,
In a circle of pain and blood.

If you cowered and refused to fight,
The derision that followed was worse
Than the beating you would've taken
If you had stayed in that circle,
Closed your eyes, and punched it out.

If you refused to fight, you became a stooge,
Subject to the whims of everyone,
Your butter and dessert taken away
By anyone who wanted to have it,
And punched by everyone
without pity.

But if you put up a good fight,
Whether you were beaten or not,
You shook the hand of your opponent,
Got pats on the back from your peers,
And walked with your head held high.
This was the unwritten code of the "Mission boys,"
And we all lived and survived by it.

And never, never did you "squeal"
To a priest or prefect if you were beaten,
Because this was the lowest you could sink.

Sometimes you won and sometimes you lost,
But you always fought the best you could,
Because that ring of boys surrounding you,

Was your judge, jury and executioner
Inside the circle, or out, you were part of it.

THE GAMES

Whenever Mission boys and girls get together,
It doesn't matter what your station in life,
Your education, profession or age,
The conversation always drifts
To those years spent at the Mission.

The conversations begin,
"Do you remember...?"
And then we take turns reminiscing
About the "rugged" games we played,
The pranks we shared, the beatings we took,
And above all, the laughs that brightened our days.

We had a game we played on swings.
One guy pumped for the sky, reaching height,
While the other sat on the seat,
Waiting for the right final moment,
To leap from the seat as far as he could.

Marks were etched in the ground,
To show the records of the past,
And the daredevils risked life and limb
To leap farther, swing higher and surpass
The records that were there to claim.

One didn't always land triumphantly;
Ask my good friend, Frosty, about this.

He fell from the seat, hit the ground,
Just in time to catch the full blow
Of the swing ricocheting on his ear.

We fell from trees into thorn bushes,
Got hit on the head with rocks,
Fell in heaps from the "monkey bars,"
Got clobbered with wood bats.
But that was the nature of the games we played.

VISITORS

One day a black basketball team came,
We all gathered around,
Our jaws agape,
We'd never seen a real live black person,
And we stared in awe.
But then we noticed
That they were staring real hard at us,
And that's when we all started laughing,
Because we realized,
At the same time
They realized,
That although we had never seen a real live black person,
They had never seen a real live Indian either!

The priests and brothers used to have family visitors,
And they showed us off like prize mules.
But even then the humor crept in.
A new priest had visitors,
His mother, father, and sister
Came all the way from St. Louis.

Here's the conversation overheard
By an alert Mission boy...

"How do you like working amongst all these Indians?"
"Oh, I really enjoy it,
And I believe the kids really like me."
"That's good."
"In fact, they have a nickname they have given me,
An Indian name.
It really makes me happy when they call me this,
In fact, every time they see me coming, they
Shout in unison. They call me 'OO-A-LA.' "

We had a real good laugh over this,
Because in Lakota, "OO-A-LA" means
"Here he comes" or "Let's scram."
"On the lookout, he's coming!"

But visitors' days were good
When our families came.
They'd pull up in old cars
Held together with baling wire,
Or in old wagons pulled by teams of horses,
And they'd pitch tents,
And camp on the playgrounds.

The women in their long dresses,
With shawls over their shoulders
And red coloring on their faces,
Walked straight and tall
With pride and dignity.

The men would ride horses
And when they dismounted,

They would sit around the fires
In their blue jeans
And cowboy hats.

The thrill was hearing the drum
And the songs at night
That went on and on,
Far into the night.
And we lay in our bunks and listened,
And finally fell asleep
With a warm feeling
That many of us still cherish.

If those people out there,
Sitting by their fires,
Were so wrong in their beliefs,
As we had been taught by the Jesuits,
Why did it make us feel so good,
So safe and warm
To have them so near?

CHRISTMAS AT THE MISSION
I wasn't very big that first Christmas.
Most of the kids had gone home,
But some of us didn't.

The church was awfully strange.
You could almost hear echos.
The songs were pretty, though.
They put all of us
Into one dining room

And we got cookies
Shaped like Christmas trees,
With green stuff sprinkled on top.
And for once I ate until I was full.

We wrapped red paper around the lights
And the little boys' gym had a red glow.
The fathers and sisters told us
What a wonderful time of the year it was,
And we should be happy.

They gave us small gifts
Wrapped in fancy paper.
I took mine outside, unopened,
Threw it into a snowbank
And cried.

CHRISTMAS VACATION

Before Christmas we would stand outside the old gray boys' building at the Holy Rosary Indian Mission and watch the cars and wagons pull up. As anxious parents gathered their children for the trip back home, many of us would have the awful feeling that maybe our parents wouldn't be able to make it this year.

Usually, our fears were unfounded because most parents were as happy to have their children home for the holidays as the children were happy to be home.

But for some, that fear did become a reality. There were several boys and girls who never went home for the holidays. Until the school year ended, the boarding school was their home.

During World War II, my father got a maintenance job at what is now Ellsworth Air Force Base in Rapid City. He rented a tar paper shack

in North Rapid on Lemon Avenue. Back in those days the 700 block of Lemon Avenue was way out in the boonies. Across the alley from our house was a swamp filled with frogs. The house was heated by a wood-burning stove, light was provided by kerosene lamps and the bathroom consisted of a one-seater outhouse.

You don't know what fun is until you've had to fight your way to the outhouse in a raging blizzard with the temperature hovering at 30 below zero.

As the holiday vacation season approached, I would suddenly take more care to observe the old bus that passed by the Indian Mission on its way from Rushville, Nebraska, to Rapid City. It usually passed by in the early afternoon.

If there were people standing along the highway, the bus would stop and pick them up. Money would change hands, a ticket would be issued and the new passengers would try to find a place to sit.

One day before the start of Christmas vacation in 1943, I watched the old bus pull up on the Mission highway. A tiny, solitary figure de-bussed (as they say nowadays) and started walking toward the Mission. My heart leaped into my throat as I realized it was my mother. She had traveled all the way from Rapid City (a metropolis that seemed a thousand miles from the Mission) to pick us up for the holidays.

The Franciscan nuns let my mother spend the night at the school infirmary, and they even let us visit with her that evening. As always, my mother had brought us those special things in life to munch on, things we never could get enough of at the Mission—peanut butter, jelly and crackers.

The next day, with our cardboard suitcases securely bound by heavy twine, we stood by the Mission highway and waited for the magical bus that would take us away to freedom.

Back in those days, it was highly unusual for any of the Mission boarding school students to ride in a motorized vehicle. We ate our meals at the Mission, had a dormitory there and spent all our time there. We really didn't have much reason to travel.

This was the second year in a row my mother had come to pick my brother, sisters and me up for the holidays. Because we were not accustomed to the swing of a motor-driven vehicle, we hadn't made it past Oglala Dam (about twelve miles north of the Mission) before getting seriously carsick the year before.

This year I was bound and determined to make it back all the way to Rapid City without getting sick. As the bus pulled away from the Mission, my mother said, "Now be sure to tell me if you start getting sick so I can tell the bus driver to stop and let you off the bus."

I nodded, grimly determined to show my mother what I was made of.

I did make it about ten miles farther than the previous year; however, I waited about two minutes too long to tell my mother. The white man seated across the aisle from us said mighty unpleasant things to my mom and me as he cleaned up his shoes. The bus driver wasn't much kinder as he ordered me from the bus.

I often wonder why I always got carsick leaving the Mission and never got sick going back. Maybe it's because I was always so depressed going back that I didn't think about getting sick.

Or maybe it's because the trip back home was always such a long, long one and the trip back was always so short.

IN RETROSPECT
You probably remember differently,
Or do you?
You had senior proms and pinball machines,
And nights at home
With family
At white schools.

We had the three R's,
Reading, 'Riting, and 'Rithmetic,
Taught to the tune
Of the principal's belt.

Separated from our mothers,
Fathers, brothers and sisters,
Indoctrinated by our new
Fathers, brothers, sisters and Mother Superior.

But it wasn't all bad.
We made friends.
We shared secrets.
We gained strength
From each other.
And most important,
We gained knowledge.

No, it wasn't all bad.
But I never learned to like it.
And I ran away again,
I never returned.

I never stopped running
Until now.

I lost something at the Mission,
And this summer,
Many years later,
With trepidation,
I came back to retrieve it
So that I could
Stop running, stop reaching
Stop fearing.

And there it was,
Waiting where I had left it
On the steps of the church
I found my spirit.

PROGRESS

I saw a hippie boy in San Francisco,
Standing on a corner by the wharf,
Bib overalls, chambray shirt,
A red bandana around his neck,
Sandals of leather with tire treads,
Shaggy hair—1975.
I saw an Indian boy at the Mission,
Standing by the gym.
Bib overalls, chambray shirt,
A red bandana around his neck,
Shoes of leather with tire treads,
Shaggy hair—1945.

ESCAPE!

ESCAPE!

When Richard "Sonny" Torres and Ray Briggs arrived at Holy Rosary Indian Mission in the fall of 1951, the first thing they did was look for a way to escape.

They were city boys and looked at things a little differently than those of us who were reservation born and raised. For instance, when they saw the wire-meshed screen on the window in the big boys' recreation room, they saw an exit to freedom. I saw it as just another window.

There was nothing spontaneous about the plan they hatched to escape. First they found a way to loosen the screws on the recreation room window. Then they chose a Sunday night to make their escape.

Sunday night was the most relaxed night of the week at the Mission school. It was the night that we saw a movie in the school gymnasium. The big boys' recreation room was at the bottom of the stairway leading to the movie seats reserved for the older boys.

Taking advantage of their street-wise ways, they contacted their friend, Glen Three Stars, in Pine Ridge Village and set up a time and place for him to meet them with his car. Shortly after the movie started, I saw them approach Mr. Bryde, a Jesuit prefect, whisper in his ear and then head down the stairway to the restrooms.

No one paid much attention to them after that because we were busy enjoying the movie. After the movie we traipsed down the stairs and stopped in the recreation room to have one last smoke before bedtime. We noticed at once that the window was open and the wire screen had been pushed out. Mr. Bryde immediately called for an assembly and roll call of all students. As we lined up, I right away noticed that Torres and Briggs were gone.

I found out later that Three Stars had picked them up near the Mission highway and driven them to Rapid City. They had made a clean escape. I hated the boarding school as much as they did and knew it was time for me to plan my escape.

I had tried to escape with my friend Pete Cummings when I was in the fourth grade, but we got caught and had to take a severe whipping with a leather strap and suffer the further indignity of being deprived of the Sunday night movies for six weeks. It took a few months to work off the demerits we accumulated from our thwarted escape.

I was now in the eleventh grade, a much older and wiser guy. I knew I would never make it through the school year. My anger at the school, the system and the priests had reached a boiling point. If I stayed any longer I would have been expelled for punching a priest. So I waited two weeks after Torres and Briggs had made their run before attempting my escape.

It was a beautiful Sunday morning in early October when I put my plan into action. Sunday Mass was always a bit longer than our regular daily Mass. I figured that if I could find a way to get out of the church early in the service, I would have nearly an hour's head start before Mass ended. Or, if I got lucky, they wouldn't miss me until after breakfast when roll call was usually held.

I left the pew and told Mr. Bryde that I was really sick to my stomach and needed to go outside for a bit. He nodded his okay and out of the church I went. After getting outside I took a couple of deep breaths, looked around cautiously to make sure no one was in sight to report me, then strolled to the girls' side of the Mission and began loping down the dirt road toward the hills and freedom.

I will never forget climbing the first hill overlooking the Mission grounds and feeling like a bird about to take flight. I paused for a few minutes to catch my breath and looked back at the buildings and grounds where I had been held captive for ten years. I then took the course I had planned and headed the four miles south to Pine Ridge Village, where I hoped to hook up with Glen Three Stars.

It seems that Three Stars had become a facsimile of the Underground Railroad for escaped students from HRM. Three Stars was one of the most famous athletes ever to come out of Pine Ridge High School, or Oglala Community High School as it was called in the days of old. He set a state record in the 440-yard dash that stood for more than twenty years. He became a legend in his own right later on in life.

I found Glen's house and he hid me out for about three days. We then scraped together enough money for me to catch a bus to Rapid City. A few days later I found out that because of my successful escape, I had been expelled forever from Holy Rosary Indian Mission. What a relief that was—because I knew that I would never have to go back to that school again.

Not once in my life have I ever regretted running away from the Mission school. At that point in my life it was the bravest act I had ever committed and I never looked back. Instead of losing something I always looked upon it as a new beginning. I don't know what course my life would have taken had I remained at the Mission school, but one year later I was in the United States Navy and traveling the world.

Left to right: John Walker, Tom Brokaw, and Tim Giago. Photo was taken in Tom Brokaw's office at NBC Studios in New York in the late '80s. Inscription by Tom Brokaw: "Tim—From one Dakota journalist to another! Tom Brokaw."

Coretta Scott King looks on as Tim Giago receives the Mencken Award from Baltimore Sun publisher James Houck on September 18, 1985. Inscription by Mrs. King: "To Tim Giago. With deep appreciation for your commitment and support— Coretta Scott King."

AFTERWORD

In the back of my mind there was always the ambition to do well. Once in a while I would hear about one of my former classmates getting a good job or completing college and I would be very proud of them. I wanted to do something with my life.

After the military I went to college under the GI Bill. Although I had taken some courses in journalism, I still wasn't sure what I wanted to do. In the late 1960s I ran across a magazine published by a Cahullia Indian man named Rupert Costo, and I eventually went to work for him as an advertising sales representative in San Francisco.

Rupert gave me the desire to be a journalist. He wrote editorials that challenged the establishment, especially those who held sway over the Indian people. His editorials rattled cages and in some cases helped to bring about positive changes.

I went to work for the *Rapid City Journal* in South Dakota after working for Rupert at his *Wassaja* newspaper and then for the *Farmington Daily Times* in the Four Corners area of New Mexico.

The 1990–91 Nieman Fellows at Harvard University. Nieman Fellowships are awarded annually by the Nieman Foundation, Milwaukee Journal. Tim Giago was only the second recipient from South Dakota to ever receive this award. He is in the second row from the top, on the right.

But I never lost my desire to return home to the Pine Ridge Reservation. I knew the Oglala Lakota people at Pine Ridge desperately needed a newspaper, and I set about trying to make this a reality.

I printed the first edition of the *Lakota Times* on July 1, 1981. Soon it grew to become the largest Indian-owned weekly newspaper in America. The paper was re-named *Indian Country Today* in 1992.

Along with the responsibility came many rewards. I met people like Robert Kennedy Jr. and Caroline Kennedy. I worked with John Siegenthaler and Allen Neuharth when they were starting *USA Today*. I visited Tom Brokaw at NBC headquarters in New York City.

But more than that, I was lucky enough to be the first Native American print journalist to be selected as a Nieman Fellow to Harvard. My writing won many state and national awards, and I was inducted into the South Dakota Hall of Fame in 1994. What a wonderful life it turned out to be for me! As H.L. Mencken of the *Baltimore Sun* said about journalism many years ago, "It is really the life of kings."

Holy Rosary Mission in the 1940s.

PART II
FROM THE DISTANCE OF TIME

ABUSES AND REMEDIES

HIDING FROM THE PAIN AND THE SHAME OF ABUSE

I once heard a man of the Jewish faith say that if Jews did not have a sense of humor many more would have died in the concentration camps. He said that no matter the pain, suffering and death surrounding them, many Jews still maintained a strange sense of humor.

It would be quite a stretch to compare life at an Indian mission boarding school to the death camps run by the Nazis, but in our own way, we Indian children suffered many indignities and assaults upon our person, our culture and our spirituality. It surprises me even to this day to recall the jokes and childish humor that kept many of us from going mad. We laughed at ourselves, at our friends, and most of all we laughed at the priests and nuns. Of course, the brothers and the prefects also never knew the jokes we made up about them or the horrible nicknames we assigned to them.

But beneath this laughter there ran a vein of pain and sorrow. Some of the insufferable abuse many endured was buried deep within us. I would see that sorrow bubble to the surface whenever I spoke publicly about my school days at the Indian Mission and my audience included Indian men and women around my age. My speeches often caused tears of sorrow brought on by things remembered that had been long suppressed.

I believe many Lakota men and women are hesitant, nay reluctant, to talk about some of the more terrible aspects of school days at mission boarding schools. Oftentimes, if there was abuse involved, whether physical or sexual, there is that lingering sense of shame that usually accompanies abuse.

The Lakota culture makes children uncomfortable to speak out against their elders, even if those elders are of a different race—and this is particularly true if there is a religious person involved. Lakota children are extremely shy when it comes to speaking about an act they find shameful. They feel that it is a reflection upon them more than it is on the perpetrator.

The Catholic Church has long been quick to quash any comments made against its priests and nuns, and the very power of the Church on Indian reservations makes it an ominous presence. Having been subjected to the iron rule of the Church and strictly disciplined for any infraction, I can say there is also an element of fear involved.

To this very day the hierarchy of the Catholic Church has refused to admit or to face the fact that all kinds of abuse took place within the walls of the Indian missions. Abuse can come in many forms and the degree of severity can be great or small. For instance, telling a young child that his or her ancestors will never be allowed to enter the Kingdom of Heaven because they were not baptized in the Church is a form of abuse.

Teaching children that any religious belief or practice outside of the Catholic Church is wrong forces them to make a judgment against the spiritual beliefs of their parents or grandparents. This action can break the very tie between child and parents that is so important to the continuity of Native culture and traditions.

The shortest road to assimilation is through the children. If they are removed from the influences of their parents and grandparents, indoctrinated into a new religion, denied their own language, and then made over into the image of the white people while isolated from their traditions, culture and spirituality, they will be effectively assimilated into another culture. This was the policy of the U.S. government in collusion with the different Christian church groups.

When the children are placed in an environment that institutionalizes the body and the spirit, the door is opened to molding them into the "civilized" people envisioned by the government, using the minions of the Church as the tools and the enforcers.

But taking a child from his parents and placing him in an institution where he remains day and night also places the responsibility for his well-being in the hands of those who would incarcerate him. The institution then must take on the role of the parent or the guardian of that child. The Catholic Church had the responsibility and the obligation to protect the children forced to attend its schools.

And this is where the institution came up short. Priests, nuns, brothers and prefects traveled to the Indian reservations, often taking up residence far from home and family. Indian children had to rely upon their good intentions, but their motives were not always of the highest order. Nearly every nun, priest, brother or prefect soon became a strict disciplinarian. Although most of us felt that there were far too many disciplinarians, we soon discovered that there were not enough to protect us.

Albert Rokey, the white maintenance man who raped my sister, routinely raped young girls at the Mission school. On Sunday mornings I would see him seated amongst the nuns and brothers in the chapel with his head bowed, hands folded, and praying intently. What a bastard! What a hypocrite!

According to some of the girls, one Catholic priest at the school loved to make them sit on his lap while he felt around in inappropriate places on their bodies. I knew the priest from the time he first came to Holy Rosary as a prefect studying for the priesthood. Ironically or tragically, this pedophile has been mentioned in books written by two Indian men who believed him to be the next thing to a saint. Their glowing praise of the man turns my stomach today.

And nothing was ever done about the dormitory prefect who tried to sexually molest me. Afterward, I tried to stay as far away from this prefect as I could even in the confines of the Mission school. But—such are childhood fears—I always felt that he was watching me whenever he was around and it was very unnerving. This pedophile finished his training as a prefect, went back East to finish his studies and became a Jesuit priest. After completing his vows, he returned to Holy Rosary Mission with even more power than when he left.

I wonder how many other children suffered the same fate as my sister, her friends and other young boys. After all, we were far from home and four miles away from the nearest community. The largest city was more than one hundred miles away. For all intents and purposes, we were captives and subject to the whims of our captors.

Some of the older boys were the children of former Mission students that had been badly abused. It is said that an abused child often becomes the abuser when he or she grows up. I saw a lot of abuse on the reservation over the years and as a news reporter I had to cover many stories involving domestic abuse, rape and incest. If I were a psychiatrist I think I could have traced a lot of this abuse straight back to the mission boarding schools.

Some of the older boys often forced themselves upon the younger, smaller and most vulnerable boys. I know I wasn't the only one who witnessed this. As a boy small for my age I had to fight off some of the older boys, and why our guardians never saw this happening around them escapes me. Often the older boys held the small boys down and rubbed their bodies on them right on the floor of the little boys' gym in full view of everyone.

Bullies played a big part in why I hated the Mission school so much. These bullies were usually appointed to serve as captains of a squad of boys and the tables in the dining hall. Some of the small boys never got a cube of butter for their bread because the captains either took it from them outright or, under the pretense of being their protector, charged them for this protection by confiscating their cubes of butter. If you did something to offend the bully he could and often did strike you across the face with his fist knowing full well that you would never have the courage to report him and even if you did, nothing would happen to protect you. I saw one of my friends get hit so hard it knocked out one of his front teeth.

But, as I said, there was no such thing as turning the bully over to the prefects or Jesuit priests because they just didn't seem to care.

My older sisters told me often about the cruelty on the girls' side of the Mission. They were struck across their bare legs with leather straps for infractions. Some were taken to a dark room in the attic of the girls' building and locked up for hours. It was nothing for a nun to slap a young girl viciously across the face.

A couple of years ago I had a conference call with two nephews and a niece, all the children of my younger sister, Shirley. She had been extremely cruel to them, and they have carried the damage for a long time. I told them about how their mother had been raped and abused by that monster at Holy Rosary. We all had a good cry as I talked, and her children said, "That explains a lot of things to us about our Mom."

Many of the priests, nuns, brothers and prefects at the Mission were good men and women. They came out to the isolation of a distant Indian reservation because of their devotion to the Church. They believed that by making the children over in their own image they were helping to save them from a life of paganism and worse.

But the road to hell is paved with good intentions, as the saying goes, and the road to salvation for the priests and nuns became our road to a living hell.

SO MANY OF US WERE NOT GOOD PARENTS

I suppose we all ask ourselves in later life whether we have been good parents. The circumstances of life often predicate the summation.

I wrote a poem many years ago that spoke of life's treatment of the Indian men and women of my generation. I compared our lives to a log rushing down a mountain stream, brushing against the banks, crashing into the occasional rock, the bark of life scraped or torn as the log crashes to its destination. The log finally settles in a quiet lagoon and turns silently in the water as it reflects upon its journey.

I called the poem "The Apparition" because at the end of its journey the log experiences an epiphany. It arrives in the form of a statue many of us gazed upon in our youth as inmates at a Catholic Indian Mission boarding school. But the statue has taken human form and speaks to us in the voice of St. Theresa, The Little Flower.

The Little Flower was the statue in the church at the Holy Rosary Indian Mission that we saw every day of the nine long months we were at the boarding school each year. In my mind she was a symbol of purity and beauty, and yet she was an "apparition" that would always be beyond our reach, emotionally and spiritually.

How could we learn to love when everything around us besmirched love? We were separated from our cultural and spiritual teachers, our parents and grandparents. We were beaten physically, psychologically and emotionally for being Indian. Our culture, language and spirituality had to be stripped away so that we could become cheap imitations of our mentors, the Franciscan nuns and Jesuit priests, prefects and brothers.

To think about the girls sheltered on the other side of the Mission grounds from us was evil. If we had thoughts of love they had to be revealed in a confessional, and penance was meted out for having these thoughts so that love became intertwined with evil. The same can be said of the girls living just two hundred yards from us and yet a lifetime away.

We did not experience the opportunity to live with and share the love our parents felt for each other. Our parents and grandparents were portrayed as dinosaurs soon to be extinct. Ours was to be the life of the "new Indian" moving into the twentieth century having shed all of the reminders. We would succeed in life because everything in our past had been erased.

Of course, this was very wishful thinking on the part of the government and the missionaries. They did not realize that neither church nor state could kill the very thing that made us human—our ties to our past, our culture, our traditions and our spirituality.

But the process was deadly. It took a toll on the young Indian men and women of my generation.

I speak not for myself alone, but for the thousands of Indian men and women who struggled for years to find themselves. Many succeeded, but many failed. We went out into the world away from the Mission boarding schools lost and confused. *If we were not Indian, what were we?* We soon realized that in the real world, we were different. In South Dakota we were not accepted in the world we had been trained to become a part of. With the lack of acceptance came the terrible feelings of rejection that became the focal point of so many of our lives. Our self-esteem had been obliterated. Many of us were actually ashamed to be Indian.

But what else could we be? We turned to drink, to promiscuity, to short-lived love affairs. We didn't know the meaning of longevity in a relationship because we had lived from year to year in the shelter and the false world of the Indian Missions. Love and sex were synonymous, and since sex was terribly evil, what did that make love?

So many of us, men and women, went through so many relationships we misconstrued as love. Children became a part of that legacy and most of us did not know how to be parents. So I guess that answers the question about whether we were good or bad parents. We just didn't know how.

This all came home to me after I was a guest on the *Oprah Winfrey Show* in Chicago. We talked about the use of Indians as mascots. A young lady in San Francisco was home that day and tuned into the *Oprah* show. She saw me and immediately called her sister in Seattle. She said, "Quick, turn on *Oprah*! I think that is our father on the show."

When I divorced their mother it had not been an easy divorce. She took the children and made it difficult for me to see them. I might add here that she was not an Indian. And I was a much different person back then. She later married again, took a new name and moved to New York City. Although I tried, there was no way I could find them. New York was a good city in which to get lost. So I just got on with my life.

About one week after the *Oprah* show, I got a call at my newspaper office. The voice on the line said, "My name is Theresa and I am your daughter." We had a family reunion in Seattle and I have spent every day since then trying to make up for all of those lost years.

My daughter Denise immediately identified with her Indian side. She was already a gifted artist. I helped her to be accepted at the Institute of American Indian Arts in Santa Fe, New Mexico, and she graduated with honors. Theresa ("Terri") went on to get a degree in microbiology from the University of Montana. I was lucky enough to be at the graduation ceremonies of both of my daughters. Theresa turned out to be "The Little Flower" in my life and has given me two wonderful grandsons, Hunter and Conner. Denise turned out to be more like me: inquisitive and a sucker for causes.

I know I will spend the rest of my life trying to be the good parent I thought I could not or would never be. And that goes for the other children I am blessed to have in my life.

WHY PRIESTS, NUNS & BROTHERS HAVE SO MUCH TO CONFESS

When I was a student at Holy Rosary Indian Mission boarding school, I spent some time as an altar boy.

Altar boys got to the chapel before the rest of the boys and girls so they could prepare to serve the morning Mass. I often saw priests, nuns and brothers lined up to go to confession on those early mornings. It made me wonder what these pious souls had to confess, because I remember that many of us nine- and ten-year-olds had to think up sins to confess when we went to our weekly confessional.

I wondered what these "holy people" had to confess until the night I was ill with a fever. Still clad in my BVDs, I got out of my bunk bed and knocked on the door of the prefect on duty to ask for an aspirin. When he came back with the pills, he knelt down in front of me, put his hands around my waist and proceeded to rub his face against my body. I was horrified. I jumped back and accidentally struck in him in the face with my elbow. He released me and I fled to my bed shaking in fear. I was only nine years old and a devout Catholic boy at the time. I never mentioned this to anyone because I was too frightened and ashamed. His name was Mr. Price. He later went on to become Father Price. How many more boys did Mr. Price touch improperly?

How many times have I witnessed and heard of small boys taken to the rooms of the on-duty prefect in the late hours of the night? One priest who taught us the Latin we needed to become altar boys often doled out lemon drops and would squeeze us in very inappropriate places as he handed us the candy. Some of the boys just shrugged and felt that a slight grope for a lemon drop was not that harmful. Let's just say that we endured it because there wasn't anything we could do about it.

I am appalled that what the Indian boys and girls endured for nearly one hundred years has suddenly become front-page news all over the world. One cannot turn on television news without witnessing the unraveling of the sex scandals in the Catholic Church. The abuse splashed across the front pages and TV screens involves modest numbers of mostly white boys and girls. The number of children abused at the Indian Mission boarding schools numbered in the thousands.

In 1998, when church abuses of Indian children brought about successful lawsuits against the churches in Canada, it was non-news in the newspapers of the United States. What the hell—it was Canada and the victims were Indian. No big deal. But now it has struck at the heart of white America and it is BIG news. If the cover-up in Boston succeeded for so long, it goes without saying that the abuse of Indian children out in the Dakotas and elsewhere was concealed indefinitely.

Did you know that it took tons of courage for those Indian men and women in Canada to stand up and confess that they had been sexually abused? Did you know that it is such a taboo among the indigenous people of this land that thousands of Indian boys and girls may never step forward to talk about this abuse? But that doesn't mean it didn't happen. Until Indian men and women overcome the shame and the fear and come forward, the crime will continue to go unpunished.

Many Indian boys and girls couldn't even speak English when they were first brought to the Indian missions. They were five and six years old. They were already terrified at having been taken from their homes and families and placed in a boarding school. It was a totally foreign experience to them. In fact, many of the nuns, priests and brothers came to America from Germany and other European countries and spoke very poor English themselves. Yet one of the first things the children discovered is that they would get a slap across the face or worse if they spoke in their own Lakota tongue, even though many could not speak English. What is the name for this kind of abuse?

The Pope called the American Cardinals to come to Rome in 2002. What I observed was a Church more concerned about its own image than the health and welfare of the children who had been abused and raped.

Maureen Dowd wrote in her *New York Times* column one Sunday during this time, "As American Catholics waited and prayed for a glimmer of humility, the princes of the church strutted off to what one church official called 'other obligations,' as if there were something more pressing than the rape of children."

There are few Indian families who have not experienced the residual impact of the abuse heaped upon their friends and family members after they were victims of the rape and abuse they experienced at the hands of the missionaries sent out to save their souls. It was not only a sin, it was a crime.

And now I know why, as an altar boy, I saw priests, nuns and brothers going to confession so often. They had a lot more to confess than most of us ever realized.

Given the success of lawsuits in Canada on behalf of abused Indian children, you might have expected the same thing to happen in the Lower 48.

In fact, two men—Jeffrey Herman and Gary Frischer—did show up in Lakota country soon after, briefcases in hand, offering to file a class-action suit against the federal government and the different church groups. But only one was a lawyer and neither had solid expertise in Indian law.

And, in the words of Jennifer Ring, who directs the American Civil Liberties Union of the Dakotas, Indian law is "highly specialized…It involves a lot of areas of the law that are not commonly taught in law schools in the United States. If you look at the Constitution, one of the powers that the federal government has is, very specifically, the right to regulate affairs dealing with Indian tribes, and that is not something that applies to any other minority group. Then you go on to the treaties, interpretation of the treaties, and jurisdictional issues. There are a lot of rules that apply to Indian country that do not apply anywhere else."

Nevertheless, the class-action suit was filed on behalf of a handful of Indian people—even though Herman told one of my reporters at the time that he had never litigated a single case involving Indian law.

I am apprehensive. I have been around Indian country for a long time. I know the complexities of Indian law and the reasons why so many other attorneys have stayed away from filing a suit on behalf of the Indian people who were abused in the boarding schools.

In the end, the statute of limitations may prevent the class-action suit from going forward. This legal issue is still being researched and has yet to be settled. But I fear that even if the case can proceed, the lawyers have gone into it ill-prepared. They only get one shot, and if they miss, the loss could put an end to any future lawsuit forever.

I really do not like those who, when proven right, say, "I told you so." But in the light of what has been happening in the Catholic Church, I can only say, "I told you so."

Because I have been in the newspaper business for more than twenty-five years, I have had the privilege of having Indian women and men come to me and speak privately about the hell they experienced in the Indian Missions. They opened up to me because of the book of poetry I wrote (called *The Aboriginal Sin*) about those places.

After the book came out, the Catholic Church advised its priests at Holy Rosary Indian Mission to deny that I ever attended that school, or if I did, it was only for about six months. I had to get affidavits signed by fellow students to support the fact that I had been a student there for ten years.

My own experience over many years has taught me that there is no one as vicious as an offended Catholic parishioner, priest, nun or bishop. They can write hate letters that would make the hair on the heads of the staunchest individuals stand on end.

My weekly column appeared in the very conservative *Rapid City Journal*. Editor Jim Kuehn fought to keep my column even though it was considered to be very controversial, because it sometimes covered issues such as the abuse of Indian children at the Missions.

When Jim retired and moved on, a new editor took his place. Joe Karius, the new editor, felt that my infrequent columns about the Indian Missions amounted to "Catholic bashing," and he advised me to tone it down or risk the consequences. Rather than give in to a threat of censorship, I pulled my column from the paper.

At the time I was the only Native American writing a weekly column for any major newspaper in this country. That was even true for South Dakota, a state with a nearly ten percent Indian population.

But it wasn't just the physical abuse I wrote about—it was the abuse that most Americans do not know or talk about. It was the abuse of taking children from their parents and shearing their hair, language, spirituality, culture, traditions and all ties that connected them to their heritage. And in the end, such abuse also sheared their self-esteem and dignity.

That was the crux of the damage inflicted upon innocent children. The vestiges of that total abuse are visible even today throughout Indian country.

Who is to speak out for the thousands of Indian children who suffered the worst kind of abuse at the hands of the Catholic Church?

Many years ago when I tried to bring it to light I was attacked and discredited, and I became a non-person to the Church. When they attempted to take away from me the years I spent at the Indian Mission, they also attempted to erase my existence on this earth. What was even worse, many of the Lakota people who had converted to Catholicism looked at me as a pariah. I was an evil person who was trying to vilify their Church.

It wasn't the Church. It was the evil inflicted upon innocent Indian children by the hands of those who served it. The Church owes thousands of Indian boys and girls more than an apology.

SEPARATE, BUT FAR FROM EQUAL

There is little argument that *Brown v. Board of Education*, decided in 1954, was one of the major Supreme Court rulings of the twentieth century, but it affected only relations between blacks and whites. What about the other ethnic minorities attending segregated schools in America?

Holy Rosary Indian Mission boarding school was, and in many ways still is, a segregated school. In Texas and New Mexico there were, and still are, many schools that are nearly 100 percent Hispanic.

In the 1950s, when *Brown* was before the Supreme Court, there were only two kinds of schools on nearly every Indian reservation in America: the Bureau of Indian Affairs schools, most of which were boarding schools, and the church-operated boarding schools.

The BIA schools were often poorly staffed and the teachers were more interested in bringing assimilation ideologies to the Indian students than in educating them. On the other hand, the church-controlled schools were not only teaching assimilation but actively indoctrinating the students into a religious order. Classes in catechism and how to serve as an altar boy were an active part of the school curriculum at the Catholic boarding schools.

A great deal of study time at the Methodist, Mormon and Episcopalian boarding schools on the Indian reservations was centered on the study of the Bible or the Book of Mormon.

Oftentimes the religious orders served as adoption agencies. Thousands of Indian children were shipped off to the homes of their parishioners across America. This was particularly true of the Mormon Church. This Church was guilty of taking many Navajo and Hopi children away from their parents on the false assumption that the Indian parents were so backward that they could not raise their children to be contributing members of society.

Just as happened in Australia to the Aborigines, these "stolen children" became nothing more than slave labor in the homes and farms of the adopted parents. There they were shorn of their culture, traditions, language and traditional spirituality. Those who found their way home became strangers in their own land. Most did not make it home. They died as "stolen children" or became assimilated into a society that really did not want them.

Mind you, many of the things I mention here were taking place at the very time that *Brown v. Board of Education* was being argued in the hallowed halls of the U.S. Supreme Court.

The schools on the Indian reservations were segregated and isolated. Out of sight, out of mind seemed to be the U.S. government's answer to the "Indian problem." It was the firm belief of the educators who came to the Indian reservations that if they could make the children over in their own image, they could more easily be assimilated into the mainstream and the "Indian problem" would cease to exist.

What they failed to understand is that there never was a problem until they brought the problem. Like so many mistakes that were made in the past, the "cultural imperialism" foisted upon the Indian people was not for their own good, but for the good of those who imposed it.

Public Law 93-638, The Indian Education and Self-Determination Act of 1974 that became law during the term of President Richard Nixon, reversed some of the damage that had been done by allowing tribal governments and Indian parents to have a say in how their children were educated. Prior to that they had none.

And so twenty years after *Brown*, the Indian people finally got the freedom to share in the education of their children. We've come a long way since then. We have our own school boards and there are now more than thirty tribally owned colleges across the Western United States. *Brown* meant nothing to the Indian people, but Public Law 93-638 did.

INDIAN SPIRITUALITY

RELIGIOUS FREEDOM FOR INDIANS, AT LAST

Freedom of religion. For two hundred years this expression was an oxymoron to American Indians.

Ratified on December 15, 1791, the First Amendment to the U.S. Constitution (part of the Bill of Rights) reads, "Congress shall make no law respecting an establishment of religion, or prohibiting the free exercise thereof..." To the people of the Indian nations, the amendment itself became the epitome of hypocrisy in America. A 1998 editorial in the Brookings, South Dakota, *Register* reads:

> Granted, the concepts of freedom of and from religion have not worked perfectly in this country; but we have been spared the religious wars that have plagued other nations throughout history. Unfortunately, however, we have not been spared overt and covert religious persecution here in America. Our nation was

more than 180 years old before we were religiously tolerant enough to put a Catholic in the White House in 1960.

Try 202 years. It was not until August 11, 1978, that Congress passed the American Indian Freedom of Religion Act.

The Act was passed as Public Law 95-341 during the 95th Congress. American Indians, led by the National Congress of American Indians, a lobby organization founded in 1944 and based in Washington, D. C., had presented many resolutions over the years to no avail. Though thwarted time and again, the members of NCAI refused to give up the fight.

For the most part, the religious practices of American Indians had been condemned by the federal government. The sacred Sundance of the Lakota had been banned. Wicasa Wakan (Holy Men) were often arrested and incarcerated for "inciting violence" when they attempted to practice certain spiritual rites of their people.

When a new spiritual practice introduced by a Paiute Holy Man named Wovoka spread across the Western United States in the late 1800s, its passion created such a fear amongst the white settlers that it eventually led to the slaughter of the innocents at Wounded Knee on December 29, 1890. The religion was known as "The Ghost Dance."

Most students can quote verbatim from the Constitution of the United States and the Bill of Rights. Here now is the Joint Resolution American Indian Religious Freedom Act:

Whereas the freedom of religion for all people is an inherent right, fundamental to the democratic structure of the United States and is guaranteed by the First Amendment of the United States Constitution;

Whereas the United States has traditionally rejected the concept of a government denying individuals the right to practice their religion and, as a result, has benefited from a rich variety of religious heritages in this country;

Whereas the religious practices of the American Indian (as well as Native Alaskan and Hawaiian) are an integral part of their culture, tradition and heritage, such practices forming the basis of Indian identity and value systems;

Whereas the traditional American Indian religions, as an integral part of Indian life, are indispensable and irreplaceable;

Whereas the lack of a clear, comprehensive, and consistent Federal policy has often resulted in the abridgement of religious freedom for traditional American Indians;

Whereas such religious infringements result from the lack of knowledge of the insensitive and inflexible enforcement of Federal policies and regulations premised on a variety of laws;

Whereas such laws were designed for such worthwhile purposes as conservation and preservation of natural species and resources but never intended to relate to Indian religious practices and, therefore, were passed without consideration of their effect on traditional American Indian religions;

Whereas such laws and policies often deny American Indians access to sacred sites required in their religions, including cemeteries;

Whereas such laws at times prohibit the use and possession of sacred objects necessary to the exercise of religious rites and ceremonies;

Whereas traditional American Indian ceremonies have been intruded upon, interfered with, and in a few instances banned;

Now, therefore, be it Resolved by the Senate and House of Representatives of the United States of America in Congress assembled, that henceforth it shall be the policy of the United States to protect and preserve for American Indians their inherent right of freedom to believe, express, and exercise the traditional religions of the American Indian, Eskimo, Aleut, and Native Hawaiians, including but not limited to access to sites, use and possession of sacred objects, and the freedom to worship through ceremonial and traditional rites.

SEC. 2. The President shall direct the various Federal departments, agencies, and other instrumentalities responsible for administering relevant laws to evaluate their policies and procedures in consultation with Native traditional religious leaders in order to determine appropriate changes necessary to protect and preserve Native American religious and cultural rights and practices. Twelve months after approval of this resolution, the President shall report back to Congress the results of his evaluation, including any changes which were made in administrative policies and procedures, and any recommendations he may have for legislative action.

Approved August 11, 1978.

There have been many challenges to this act since 1978. The use of the eagle feather, peyote, sacred sites (such as Devil's Tower in the Lakota Black Hills), and of American Indian prayers in schools have all been either challenged or scrutinized. The Act was a major step to protect the spiritual beliefs and practices of all American Indians.

Just as most Americans are familiar with other Acts to protect their freedom of religion, I hope you read this Act and know that many American Indians fought long and hard to see it to fruition. It took more than two hundred years.

TURNING BACK TO TRADITIONAL INDIAN SPIRTUALITY

For a long time, I was a recovering Catholic.

I didn't choose that religion; it was chosen for me. I didn't choose to have a first Communion, to attend catechism classes, to be confirmed or to be an altar boy. My parents were Catholic and so it was handed down to me.

I rejected Catholicism many years ago. It didn't happen as a great revelation, but it happened over many years of observation. It happened as I became educated to the many things the Catholic Church did to destroy by indoctrination the culture and spirituality of the American Indian.

Many traditional holy men lost their powers and their accepted place in the tribe at the behest of the Catholic and Protestant missionaries. If there is an Indian student who attended an Indian mission school in the

1940s who cannot remember the priests and nuns telling us about the evils of Indian medicine men and of other religions, they have very short and selective memories.

The missionary boarding schools used religion as the tool to "civilize" the indigenous children. The idea was that if the natural spirituality of the children was destroyed and replaced through the indoctrination of Christianity, the children would be saved—not only intellectually, but also spiritually.

The ancient spiritual beliefs of the indigenous children, beliefs that had been passed from generation to generation for centuries, were discarded by the priests and preachers as something evil, something akin to paganism. The approach was to kill the "heathen spirit" and replace it with a Christian spirit. This religious immersion came in the form of Jesus Christ, the apostles and all of the saints. Now these were spiritual symbols the religious teachers felt that all Indian children would embrace without question.

In many cases they were right. Soon they were sending American Indian preachers out amongst their own people in an effort to turn them away from their ancient spiritual practices toward the now widely accepted principles of Christianity.

Some of these Catholic Indians believe that we "reformed Catholics" do not have the right to be critical of an institution that attempted to indoctrinate us against ourselves and our people. Worse than that, some even believe that if we did not embrace Catholicism, we did not amount to a "hill of beans" in our lives.

There are many Lakota people who went out into the world and got an education without the security blanket of the Catholic Church. Many of us came back home to see what we could do for the betterment of our own people. We didn't come back as missionaries. We came back as concerned citizens of the Oglala Lakota Nation, the Sicangu Nation, the Navajo Nation, etc. We didn't know what we could do to help, but we tried.

Many of us also turned back to the traditional spirituality of our ancestors. We turned to holy men like Rick Two Dogs to re-educate us and to return to us that which the different churches had stolen from us. Many Navajo rebelled against the Mormon Church, which was predominant in their geographic location, and returned to their traditional teachers. Many Indians who would chide me for writing about the Indian Missions were blind to the abuses heaped upon the Indian children at mission boarding schools.

At the Mission schools, students went to Mass seven days a week, said Hail Marys aloud and in unison hundreds of times a week, and were rapped on the head with a heavy key ring for not paying attention. On our own, many of us discovered the calm and sincerity of our traditional spirituality. Hell and brimstone were not a part of the Lakota spirituality. We learned from joy, not fear.

Traditional spirituality is not a once-a-week thing. Some ceremonies, the Sundance for example, last four consecutive days. I know of Lakota men and women who were fired from their jobs for taking time off for the annual Sundance. Would they have been fired if they went to a Catholic retreat for four days?

Often Lakota ceremonies such as the *yuwipi* last late into the night or all of the night. All participants accept this without question. There is no clock to tell the participants when a ceremony should start or when it should end. Time is what the white man brought to the Lakota.

As a newspaper editor always on a deadline, time has become a friend and an enemy. But if any of my employees want to attend a traditional ceremony, I always give them the freedom to do so.

I recall that one Ojibwe Indian man incarcerated in the South Dakota State Prison was denied the right to attend his grandmother's funeral because, according to the warden, "she was not a close relative." The *unci* (grandmothers) are revered in nearly every Indian tribe in America. They are often the teachers and the acting parents of the little ones.

This is a concept that goes way over the head of many non-Indians. An aunt or an uncle is often an important figure in a traditional Lakota family. In the old days, when a father died, his brother would take the responsibility for his children. He literally became their father and his children became brothers and sisters to those of his deceased brother.

When my employees lose an aunt or an uncle, they are always allowed the time off to attend the wake and funeral.

There are those Native Americans who committed themselves totally to the religions they borrowed from the European settlers. It is their choice. There are also those who found their religion at the Indian mission boarding schools and that is also their choice.

But there are many Lakota people who have turned their backs upon the religions that were forced upon them by Christian do-gooders who sought to "kill the Indian to save the child." They believed they were doing this for our own good. Thankfully, many of our traditional ancestors took their beliefs underground and emerged when Indians were finally granted religious freedom by an Act of Congress in 1978.

It's taken me nearly a lifetime to shake the indoctrination foisted upon me by the Catholic Church, but now I am fully recovered.

THE SIOUX TRIBES AND THE GREAT SUNDANCE

Before I proceed let me give a little background on the Great Sioux Nation. While many tribes are actually included in the designation "Sioux," they can be divided into three different dialect goups. They are different because of the use of the letters "L," "D" and "N." In other words, where the Lakota use an "L" the Dakota use a "D" and the Nakota use an "N." For example, Lakota say "friend" as "kola." Dakota say "koda" and Nakota say "kona."

Tribes speaking Dakota include the Santee, made up of the Wahpekute, Mdewakantonwan and Wahpetonwan (or Wahpeton), and the Sisitonwan (or Sisseton). The Yankton (made up of the Ihanktonwan and the Ihanktonwanna) speak Dakota and Nakota. Speaking Lakota are the Titonwan (or Teton—a corruption of the word for "People of the Prairie"), consisting of the Oglala (Pine Ridge), Brule (Lower Brule and Rosebud), Hunkpapa (Standing Rock), Mniconjou, Sans Arc and Two Kettle (Cheyenne River) and the Rosebud Brule who call themselves Sicangu.

Tribes speaking dialects derived from the so-called Siouan dialect are many. They include the Winnebago, Iowa, Omaha, Ponca, Oto, Missouri, Kaw, Osage, Quapaw, Catawba, Biloxi, Ocanechee and Tuteh. I recall attending a powwow on the Osage Nation several years ago and finding myself quite surprised to be able to understand many of the words spoken by the Osage.

The last weeks in June and the early weeks in July are the time many branches of the tribes called Sioux celebrate their most sacred ritual: the Sundance.

When this most sacred ceremony was outlawed by the United States many years ago, the holy men of the different tribes took the ceremony underground. It would be held far away from prying eyes in the Badlands (*Maka Sica*) or way out in the plains away from the white settlements.

I find it ironic that those immigrants who came to this country seeking freedom of religion would prohibit the indigenous people from practicing their spirituality. Pete Swiftbird (now deceased), one of the last *Heyoka* (clown, contrary, a holy person who did everything contrary to the norm), told me long ago that American holidays such as the Fourth of July proved to be analogous to the secret incorporation of Lakota religious rituals.

While the Bureau of Indian Affairs leaders were busy holding American ceremonies and parades and giving speeches, the Lakota would sneak in some of their traditional dances and ceremonies. Of course, the white leaders looked upon these ceremonies, songs and dances as quaint and even nostalgic, but they never knew that the wool was being pulled over their eyes.

When at last the American Indian Religious Freedom Act made it legal to participate in the Sundance again, ceremonies could be held more openly. While this made participation easier and more widespread, it had the unforeseen and somewhat unfortunate consequence of making it accessible to those who would exploit the ceremony without real understanding of its meaning and the traditions behind it.

The very traditional Sundances are for the members of the tribe only. No cameras or non-Indians are allowed, yet several Sundances over the past twenty years have been open to all comers and cameras were even allowed into the ceremonies. Of course, this goes against all that is sacred to the traditional Lakota.

But, I suppose like so many things since the advent of television and MTV, nothing is sacred. It seems to me that the spirituality of so many Indian tribes has become diluted by overexposure and by flagrant abuse by wannabes, false shamans and New Agers. One well-known Indian educator even held a Sundance that was attended by many non-Indians as a sort of workshop or as a reward for contributions given to his organization.

There is also the problem of one tribe after another adopting the ceremonial practices of other tribes. The sacred Sundance has been held in New Mexico, where no tribe ever included it in any traditional rituals, and in other parts of the country. The Navajo conduct a Sundance at Big Mountain, a section of land once held by the Navajo that was partitioned by the federal government and returned to the Hopi Nation. The Sundance was never a Navajo ceremony. Why they would want to usurp and claim one of the most sacred ceremonies of the tribes of the Northern Plains is puzzling. To the traditional Lakota this is akin to blasphemy. It is said by the *wicasa wakan* (holy men) that bad will come to those who desecrate their traditional spirituality.

There are many Indians who do not like to see public displays of their spirituality. I always use "spirituality" to describe the sacred rites of an Indian tribe because to use the word "religion" would not be correct. A religion is structured as an organized faith that is practiced within the pages of a written document such as a Bible or Quran. The "spirituality" of the Indian nations is one of absolute freedom that has no dogmatic guidelines.

By public display, I mean those times when the prayers of the Indian spiritual leader are performed in front of a mixed audience. Other Indians have told me that they are embarrassed when a spiritual leader prays in his own language to an audience of non-Indians incapable of understanding what he is saying.

For the most part the audience stands in reverence, with heads bowed and hands clasped in front of them. In the old days the Lakota never stood with head bowed when they prayed. The stood with arms outstretched and heads held high as they prayed to the sky where *Wakan Tanka* (Great Spirit) dwelled.

It seems that Indians cannot have a convention without calling upon a local medicine man to say a prayer in a language none of them understand. The prayer is always said from the rostrum before the start of the convention. Sometimes the prayer is longer than the keynote address that is about to follow. This causes the non-Indian audience to shift from foot to foot in an effort to remain respectful.

I've even heard non-Indian audiences applaud after the medicine man completes his prayer, as if to say, "Jolly good show, old bean!" And that is what it often turns out to be, just a good show for an audience wanting to have "an Indian experience."

The next convention I stage will be held differently. I will ask that the Indian people gather in a private place where they can share a prayer with a Holy Man prior to going to the convention floor. In this way our spirituality is kept to ourselves and not put on public display.

Some elders also are bothered by all of this public display of spirituality. I have heard them say, "The white man took everything that once belonged to us and now they want to take our spirituality." Of course, this is always followed by, "This is the one thing we have left and it is the one thing that we must keep for ourselves only."

In a way, I feel sorry for those Indian people who have embraced the religion of the invaders. How can they worship a God that was brought over from another world? There are those who say we all worship the same God, so what difference does it make what our religion is? I believe an impartial observer of the Hindu, Muslim, Jewish, or Christian faith would find that hard to swallow. If people worship the same God, then why are they killing each other because of their religious differences?

Embracing the religion of the white man did not save the lives of those Indians slaughtered in the name of the new God they had just embraced.

The traditional Lakota know where to go for their annual Sundance. They know it will be closed to all outsiders and they know that the *wicasa wakan* conducting the ceremony are traditionalists to the core and have trained for many years to be able to hold this most sacred ceremony. One *wicasa wakan* that I know of can trace the holy men in his family back five hundred years.

The same can be said of the most guarded ceremonies of some of the Pueblo people of New Mexico and the Hopi of Arizona. Perhaps these tribes may put on a show of a ceremony for the general public during the tourist season, but the true and sacred ceremonies are always held in secret, outside of the prying eyes of the non-member and non-Indian.

The purpose of the Sundance is for the members participating to sacrifice through pain, prayer and endurance for the future of their people. The ritual takes place over a four-day period. The dancers enter the *inipi* (sweatlodge) prior to the ceremony for purification.

Their breasts are pierced with small pieces of cherry wood attached to leather thongs that are tied to the Sundance pole. The pole at the center of the dancers is sacred. The dancers dance four days, and on the final day they fall back and break away from the pole, tearing the cherry wood from their chests.

It takes great courage and stamina to complete this ceremony in its entirety. Many of the dancers have talked about how the ceremony changed them forever. Most broke away from Christianity and dedicated their lives to serving their people. They became non-smokers and non-drinkers and devoted themselves to their families.

The spirituality of the Indian people should once more be taken to a secret place. There should be no more of this "Indians on parade" mentality to start a convention.

If the true spirituality of the Lakota, Hopi, Pueblo, Blackfeet, Crow, Navajo, Inupiat or any other Indian nation of the Western hemisphere is to mean anything to the Indian people themselves, it must be taken back from those who stole it, abused it and made fun of it. Indian spirituality is not a commodity that can be bought or sold. It is not something that can be brought out into the light like a flag only when it needs to be waved. Nor is it something that can be imitated by pretenders.

It is something that is deep, profound, sensuous, mysterious, ancient and unfathomable. It is the one thing we still own that cannot be given away, shared or taken from us.

Once our spirituality is gone, we no longer exist as a distinct people.

Holy Rosary Mission in the 1940s.

EPILOGUE

DEMOLITION

It was Sunday morning and the campus grounds around Holy Rosary Mission were deserted. I could hear the church choir singing in the distance and the melody seemed to hang in the early autumn air.

I was walking along a dirt road behind the Mission with my eight-month-old son, Timmy, perched on my shoulders. As we passed the old poultry farm my son waved wildly as he spotted a fat, lazy magpie bouncing through the limbs of a nearby tree. The chattering of the bird, the smell of the grass and the familiar sights along the dirt road brought back a flood of memories.

As a boy I had walked this road many times and it struck me as ironic that I was strolling today with my son. Many, many years ago my father Tim walked this very road when he was a student at Holy Rosary.

I recalled that old Jim Iron Cloud walked up to me at the Sioux Nation Shopping Center store in Pine Ridge Village. He said, "Young Tim, your father and me were very good friends when we were small boys. One time at Holy Rosary we got our behinds blistered for speaking in our Lakota language."

As he took my hand, Mr. Iron Cloud gazed into the distance as if he were recalling the times long past. He said, "Your father was a good man." Coming from this respected elder his words meant so much to me.

My father had departed Holy Rosary when Red Cloud Hall was constructed in 1921. And now Red Cloud Hall is gone, crushed by the demolition ball and carted away in trucks. The hall had been our home. Its third floor was our dormitory, the second floor our classrooms, and the first floor our gymnasium and playroom.

A bright new building stands in its place. There are no more dormitories, only classrooms. Although the cold, gray concrete building has been destroyed, the memories are still there.

The school itself has undergone an evolution of sorts. Whenever I see the beaming faces of the young, white volunteers who teach the Lakota children at Holy Rosary, I wonder why they have left their homes in the East to come out here to the Pine Ridge Reservation. Do they know how it used to be here? Do they consider their stint on the reservation penance or are they here to really help the children?

Do they know of the long and sordid history of the involvement of the Catholic Church, in collusion with the government of the United States, to demolish the entire culture of the Indian children by whatever means?

Do they know that the children were taught that the only way to succeed in life was to abandon the reservation and take up the life of the white man? Do they know that we should have been taught and encouraged to stay home and make the reservation a better place?

Although Red Cloud Hall is no longer, in the minds of those still alive, the survivors of the Indian Mission boarding school, it will always be a part of our history and its destruction must not cause it to be lost.

The policy of the Church to assimilate and acculturate a people into the mainstream of America regardless of the methods or the consequences was the policy of man, not God. Although it was carried out in the name of God, it was steeped in the frailties of humans.

Those who came to our reservation to educate us so that we would no longer be Indians had the best of intentions.

It's just that they never asked us if this is what we wanted.

FINAL NOTES

The boarding school experiment that lasted for nearly a hundred years brought about more harm than good to the Indian people. The experiment reached across Indian country and affected the lives of thousands of Indian children.

It has only been since the 1970s that the Indian people have had an opportunity to create an educational system on the reservations that is compatible with their culture, traditions and spirituality.

Left to their own devices, the Indian people have struggled mightily to put behind them a system that was intended to destroy rather than build. It has not been an easy challenge. Often it is easier to start from scratch rather than to amend, change, or restructure an educational system already in place. And this is what the Indian teachers and administrators face today.

Even Holy Rosary Mission—now Red Cloud Indian School—has made every effort to change. They have incorporated the teaching of the Lakota language into the curriculum and have placed a special emphasis on teaching the real history of the Indian people.

This is a complete reversal of the school's early policies. Because of the transition, Red Cloud Indian School has become one of the finest schools on the Pine Ridge Reservation. Coming from me, that is quite an admission and what is more, a compliment I believed I was incapable of making.

There is still hostility toward me at Red Cloud, and that may be because it is much more difficult for the Catholic Church to admit guilt than to express forgiveness. Although individual Catholic priests, many of them former instructors at Indian mission boarding schools, have expressed sorrow and remorse to me for their participation in the boarding school experiment, the administrators at Red Cloud have never apologized. Instead they have "circled the wagons" in an effort to conceal and protect a system that has proved wrongheaded.

Although I have been the commencement speaker at nearly every Indian high school in South Dakota, I have never been invited to speak at Holy Rosary Mission, a school where I spent a little more than ten years of my life.

I have received many awards for my accomplishments as a writer, journalist, newspaper editor and publisher. This should be a source of pride to Holy Rosary Mission. Yet because I spoke out against a failed system that did severe damage to so many Indian children, the mere mention of my name at Red Cloud will provoke caustic comments from the school staff and administrators. "Well, he never graduated from here," is one of the most common put-downs flung in my direction.

No, I did not graduate from Holy Rosary Mission, but I did spend the better part of my school days there. And I do believe that the education I received there helped me to pursue the ventures in life that have made me what I am today.

Reconciliation and forgiveness can be likened to a two-way street. I have acknowledged the dramatic changes that have taken place at Holy Rosary and I praise the efforts of those who made them, though I think they would not have made them so readily if not for a push in the back from other Lakota and me.

The Church and its school administrators have to grow up. They cannot deny that I ever attended school there, nor can they continue to deny the accomplishments I have made in my life after Holy Rosary.

In many ways Holy Rosary served as a source of inspiration for me. No matter the hardships, some good had to come from it.

When I sat in my second-grade classroom and listened to the lessons of Sister Patricia, never in my wildest dream did I ever believe I would walk the grounds of Harvard Yard as a student at Harvard University. It was an impossible dream that came true and my ten years at Holy Rosary contributed to that achievement.

There was loneliness and pain there, but there were also nuns and priests that were wonderful teachers who instilled in my mind the thirst for learning. The first step in reconciliation is to admit wrong and apologize. I ask the Church and the school to take these steps for the sake of healing.

I met with the new Superintendent of Red Cloud Indian School, Robert Brave Heart, on March 31, 2005. Also present was the school principal, Father Peter Klinck, as well as Father Don Doll of Creighton University in Nebraska, who served as intermediary for the meeting, and Lydia Whirlwind Soldier, a former student at St. Francis Indian School on the Rosebud Indian Reservation.

I reiterated to them many of the things I have mentioned here, and I feel that the rapport was good and that the school is willing to admit to the things that happened many years ago rather than treat them as bad dreams to be swept under the rug.

Bob Brave Heart is the first Lakota ever to serve as superintendent at the school, and his father, Basil, was a classmate of mine at the Mission School. As a matter of fact, when Pete Cummings and I ran away from the Mission while we were in the fourth grade, it was Bob's grandfather who caught us and brought us back to the Mission. Life does go full circle.

As I have observed, the situation has completely changed at Red Cloud School, and it is a fine source of education on the Pine Ridge Reservation. I hope the school will start to recognize me as a former student and respect the things I have accomplished in my life. In return, I will try to work with them to promote the good things they are now doing for the reservation's Indian children.

If the school is willing to put away its denial and admit to its past wrongdoing, the staff and faculty at the Mission will have come a long way to healing the terrible wounds that have damaged so many. In the spirit of Red Cloud, Sitting Bull, Crazy Horse, Little Wound, Bull Bear, Young Man Afraid of his Horses, American Horse, Gaul and all the other courageous and wise chiefs of the Great Sioux Nation, I ceremoniously bury the hatchet of contention between Holy Rosary Mission and myself.

The dramatic changes in Indian education do not end with the changes at institutions like Holy Rosary, St. Francis, Marty, St. Josephs and the other Catholic Indian Missions in South Dakota. Although about half of the former students from these mission schools fell through the cracks and ended up in prison, committed suicide, became hopeless alcoholics, drug addicts or abusers of their wives and children, many moved on with their lives in more successful ways.

Among those at Holy Rosary, Sagué (Walking Stick) died a couple of years ago of throat cancer. His real name was G. Wayne Tapio, and from the mission school he went on to become a respected member of the Oglala Sioux Tribal Council and mayor of the village of Pine Ridge.

Charles Trimble, known as "Wobbie," graduated from the University of South Dakota and became the Executive Director of the National Congress of American Indians, the largest and oldest Indian organization in America. He also was one of the founders of the American Indian Press Association around 1974. The AIPA went belly up after a short life because of its inability to secure funding. However, it was an idea that happened before its time.

"Wobbie" was my classmate and my friend. It was his inspiration that led me to start the Native American Journalists Association in 1984, just 10 short years after AIPA folded. NAJA will celebrate its 21st anniversary this year.

P-2 was really Aloysius Black Tail Deer. He worked for many years as a gifted artist and craftsman for Sioux Pottery in Rapid City. He died several years ago of an acute case of diabetes.

Buck Jones was killed in Korea. Tiny Tim was really Leo Wounded Foot. He also carried another nickname: Brown Bomber. He died several years ago and I never found out what his course in life took.

As far as I know Rochester is still living on the Pine Ridge Reservation. His first name I forget but his last name was Red Elk. Magpie, Melvin White Magpie, died in prison. Sioux Boy, Leo Her Many Horses, pursued a career in education and he passed away several years ago.

Omaha, Louis Pretty Boy, was roaming the streets of Pine Ridge bumming money for alcohol the last time I saw him. He died about six years ago.

Curly Bill, Melvin Irving, also passed away several years ago, as did Fatty, Snazzy, Dillinger and Plum. "Snazzy" was really Albert Trimble. He went on to a successful career with the Bureau of Indian Affairs and then he returned to the Pine Ridge Reservation, where he ran for the presidency of the tribe and won. He was responsible for securing the funds to build all of the community centers scattered around the different districts on the reservation. He also had a beautiful building constructed near Kyle on the reservation to serve as the new headquarters of the Oglala Sioux tribal government. An election to move the government failed and Tom Shortbull later secured the building and it became the center for the Oglala Lakota College.

Left to right: Tim Giago, Robert Kennedy, Jr., and John Walker. This photo was taken in the late '80s at Robert Kennedy's home in White Plains, New York.

Plum, Gerald Clifford, went on to be the youngest person ever to graduate from the South Dakota School of Mines and Technology. He formed a consulting organization called ACKO, Inc. and was responsible for taking the law enforcement out of the hands of the Bureau of Indian Affairs on the Pine Ridge Reservation and putting it under the control of the tribal government.

Duane Garnette is now a retired rancher. He lives on the Garnette family allotment near Potato Creek on the Pine Ridge Reservation. His brother, James W. Garnette, known as "Heavy," is also retired after serving as a Deacon with the Catholic Church.

Father Edwards, "Eddie Boy," died several years ago of Alzheimer's disease. Father Fagin and Sister Peakie (Sister Helenita) have also passed away.

It seems that so many of the boys and girls and priests, nuns and brothers I wrote about many years ago have all gone on to meet their maker. They took their memories, the good and the bad, of Holy Rosary Indian Mission to their graves.

In addition, former boarding school students like Peter MacDonald of the Navajo Nation and Lionel Bordeaux of the Rosebud Reservation opened the doors for institutions of higher education right on the lands of the Indian reservations.

What started out as Navajo Community College (now Diné College) on the Navajo Nation led the way for the many Indian colleges that followed. Bordeaux was instrumental in building Sinte Gleska (Spotted Tail) University on the Rosebud Reservation and Tom

Allen Neuharth, founder of *USA Today*, and Tim Giago, then editor of the *Lakota Times*, during a Neuharth visit to the newspaper at Rapid city.

Shortbull, an Oglala Lakota man, helped build the Oglala Lakota College on the Pine Ridge Reservation with a branch in Rapid City.

Colleges controlled by Indian school boards have sprung up on many Indian reservations in America. Currently there are thirty-six Indian colleges located on Indian reservations from South Dakota to Arizona. These colleges have opened the doors for a higher education degree for many Indians who would not have gone on to college.

When Public Law 93-638, the Indian Education and Self-Determination Act, passed during the Nixon administration, it changed the way schools operated on the Indian reservations forever.

For the first time in the history of Indian education, the people were given the opportunity to form school boards and to have input into the way education courses were structured at their schools. Prior to that, the parents of Indian students had no voice, and organizations like Parent–Teacher associations were unknown on Indian reservations.

It has been a long and arduous educational process for the tribal leaders and educators. First they had to recognize that they now had a say in how their children were educated—as well as a say in how the money allocated to the schools was spent. This was entirely new, so it was no surprise that people made mistakes. Many times the educators and tribal leaders had to go back to the drawing board to correct those mistakes.

Left to right: Wendell Chino, Chairman of the Mescalero Apache, Tim Giago, and Roger Jourdain, Chairman of the Red Lake Band of Ojibwe. Photo was taken in 1987 when the three met to discuss the Indian Gaming Regulatory Act of 1988.

With the success of so many Indian casinos, some tribes have used these new funds to rebuild their schools and to bring in better superintendents and principals. Many have used the casino revenues to set aside funds for scholarships. Never before in the history of tribal governments have so many children from the Indian reservations had the opportunity to pursue degrees in higher education.

Breaking the shackles of colonialism and church authority in Indian education has been an uphill battle, but it has definitely turned in favor of the Indian nations. Many of the schools once operated by the Catholic Church, for one, have been turned over to the tribal governments. Even schools like Holy Rosary Mission (now Red Cloud Indian School) have turned over some of the decision–making to tribal members.

With the advent of crack cocaine and methamphetamine cutting a wicked path through Indian country, the school systems on the reservations are even more important. The dropout rate on some reservations is still much too high, and suicide among Indian teenagers is still more than three times above the national average.

Tim Giago (far left), Conroy Chino (now New Mexico's Secretary for the Department of Labor) and Peggy Berryhill (recent founder of the Native Media Resource Center) receive Media Persons of the Year awards at the National Indian Media Convention in Phoenix, Arizona, in 1982.

Indian educators and the parents of the children must put their heads together and find some way to solve these new problems. Educating children of every race is one of this nation's priorities, and although the problems facing the children living on Indian reservations are quite different from those attending schools in an urban setting, in the long run they are the same. Keeping children in school and providing them with a safe and secure opportunity to excel is happening even as I write this. It's been more than a hundred years in the making, but perhaps we can now see an end to the dreadful impact the misguided boarding schools have had on three generations of Indian children.

I will always believe that in order to know where we are going we must first know where we have been, and as one of the survivors of the boarding school system, I will not let the teachers of today forget the past. My generation was one of the last of the boarding school era and we are fast dying off, but our memories are still fresh and oftentimes troubled by the experiences we endured as children.